Dark Angels

The First Legion, the Unforgiven, the Sons of the Lion

Contents

Written by: Jeremy Vetock. Cover Art: Raymond Swanland.

Art, Design, Production and Reprographics by the Games Workshop Design Studio

Special thanks to our playtesters: Nick Bayton, John Bracken, Stefano Carlini, Paul Hickey, Matt Hilton, Trevor Larkin, Gary Shaw, Adam Snook

British Cataloguing-in-Publication Data. A catalogue record for this book is available from the British Library.

UK
Games Workshop Ltd,
Willow Rd, Lenton,
Nottingham,
NG7 2WS

NORTHERN EUROPE
Games Workshop Ltd,
Willow Rd, Lenton,
Nottingham,
NG7 2WS

NORTH AMERICA
Games Workshop Inc,
6211 East Holmes Road,
Memphis,
Tennessee 38141

AUSTRALIA
Games Workshop,
23 Liverpool Street,
Ingleburn,
NSW 2565

Introduction

The Dark Angels stand at the forefront of Humanity's defence, and few can match their long history of triumphs. This utter dedication to war in the Emperor's name is despite, or perhaps even because of, the sinister failings of their secret past.

Engulfed in an escalating epoch of total war, the galaxy-spanning Imperium of Mankind is beset on all sides. Only through constant vigilance and unremitting war does humanity ward off extinction, and of all the forces of the Imperium, none fight with more grim determination than the battle brothers of the Dark Angels Space Marines. They do not seek glory or the adulation of the masses, but are instead consumed with punishing transgressions and delivering the Emperor's vengeance. No matter the foe, no matter the odds, the Dark Angels stubbornly refuse to accept defeat. However, behind their roll call of victories and the façade of their steady disposition lies a dark obsession. Haunted by their past, they are wholly dedicated to their war of redemption, relentlessly fulfilling their secret crusade.

Within this tome can be found the truth about the Dark Angels' shadowy past. These pages reveal an epic tale of betrayal and tragedy. Best of all, you can join the most brooding and gothic of Space Marine Chapters in their ongoing war, but will your quest for vengeance lead to atonement or cross the line into eternal damnation?

WARHAMMER 40,000

If you are reading this codex, then you have already taken your first steps into the Warhammer 40,000 hobby. The Warhammer 40,000 rulebook contains all the rules you need to fight battles with your Citadel miniatures, and every army has its own codex that acts as a definitive guide to collecting and unleashing it upon the tabletop battlefields of the Warhammer 40,000 universe. This codex allows you to turn your collection of Dark Angels Space Marines into an unstoppable strike force ready to continue its wars of redemption.

DARK ANGELS SPACE MARINES

The Dark Angels are feared by foes and allies alike. To the all-round power and versatility of the Space Marines, the Dark Angels add grim tenacity and two unique fighting companies - the highly mobile Ravenwing and the Terminator squads of the Deathwing. They will appeal to anyone seeking a powerful force, driven by a need to atone for their sinister and gothic past.

HOW THIS CODEX WORKS

Codex: Dark Angels contains the following sections:

- **The Dark Angels:** The first section introduces the Dark Angels, including their origins, the Fall of their homeworld of Caliban, and the secrets of their dark heritage. A history of their many battles for redemption follows.

- **The Unforgiven:** All the characters, units and vehicles available to the Dark Angels Space Marines are examined here. Each unit's entry covers its role on the battlefield, its rules and any unique skills it has.

- **Armoury of the Rock:** This section contains full details and rules for the weapons, armour and equipment used by the Dark Angels and their Successor Chapters.

- **Sons of the Lion:** This section contains a stunning selection of Citadel miniatures from the Dark Angels Space Marines range. From single models to vast armies, this showcase is sure to inspire your collection.

- **Angels of Death:** The army list takes all of the units shown in the Unforgiven section and arranges them, with their points value, so you can choose an army for your games.

THE DARK ANGELS

The Dark Angels were the first Legion of Space Marines, genetically modified superhuman warriors created by the Emperor himself. Since fighting at the forefront of the Great Crusade, at the dawn of the Age of the Imperium, the Dark Angels have battled against Mankind's most terrible enemies. Now, over 10,000 years later, the Dark Angels still heroically serve Mankind.

The Dark Angels are dreaded by their enemies and held in awe by those they protect. Yet despite their unsurpassed battle record, the Dark Angels are not embraced by those whom they serve. It does not take the heightened awareness of an empath to sense the brooding obsession that coils around the Chapter. They bear an unsettling mien and are forever enshrouded by myths and insinuations.

It is no surprise that there are rumours about the Dark Angels, for they are an inscrutable Chapter, cloistered within their mysterious fortress monastery upon the asteroid known as 'The Rock'. They emerge to answer the call of battle, arriving unlooked-for on battlefields across the expanse of the Imperium. They call no planet home, but crisscross the stars following a mysterious path known only to themselves.

Those who serve alongside the Dark Angels find them taciturn, wholly absorbed by their archaic battle rites, as if purposefully detaching themselves from those they fight to protect. In them there is a brotherhood and a solemnity unmatched by even the grimmest of their fellow Space Marine Chapters. Of their own agenda, the Dark Angels remain quiet as the grave. Upon completion of a mission, they disappear with the same unexpected swiftness that marked their arrival, heedless of the unease they have spread and uncaring of the rumours whispered in their wake.

THE STAIN OF HISTORY

To understand the secretive Dark Angels, we must return to a time more than 10,000 years ago, when the Emperor walked as a man, striding from a dark age of regression, superstition and subjugation. Although Mankind had once plied the stars, all links between inhabited planets were long severed. Most human populations were enthralled by xenos or lived in the ruins of their once-great civilisations. It was in this bleak era that the Emperor rose to reunite Terra, the fabled birth-planet of Mankind. To help him on his quest to reclaim the galaxy, the Emperor created the genetically-engineered superhumans known as Primarchs, although his industry and near-flawless design did not go unnoticed. A strange vortex burst forth from the Warp, whisking the still foetal Primarchs into that chaotic realm.

The twenty incubation capsules drifted in the Warp for decades, or perhaps centuries, for in that place of dread the laws of time are bent and reshaped. Eventually, the amniotic tanks re-entered realspace, scattered across the galaxy. The capsule of one Primarch, he who would become known as Lion El'Jonson, founder of the Dark Angels, was cast onto an isolated planet on the northern fringe of the Eye of Terror – a death world known as Caliban.

CALIBAN

Caliban was as harsh an environment as any in the galaxy. In the dire forests that covered the globe lived creatures warped by unnatural forces, twisted into hulking fiends that stalked the arboreal world. Despite the danger, Caliban had a human population, for it had been settled during the expansions of the Age of Technology. Cut off by Warp storms, civilisation on Caliban devolved over time into a semi-feudal state. Those that survived did so by retreating into huge fortresses located in clearings that were hacked into the all-encompassing woodlands at a great cost in lives.

The people of Caliban were a pugnacious folk, ruled over by the warrior elite. Some old technology had been preserved, and the best knights were equipped with an early form of power armour. They spent most of their energy fending off the monstrous creatures that lurked in the surrounding forest. When a particularly large or ferocious beast took up residence near a settlement, the nobles would call a quest, summoning the best warriors from all around. Slaying a quest-creature brought high honour: however, more often than not, a quest brought only a horrific death delivered by the teeth and talons of some hell-spawned abomination.

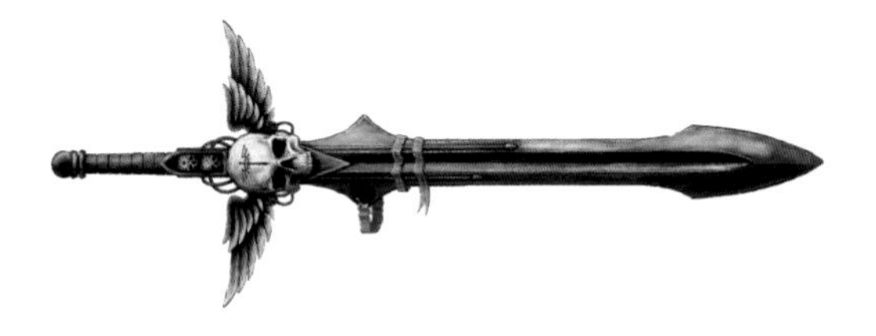

THE YOUNG LION

Most of the other Primarchs were fortunate enough to be found and raised by local human inhabitants of the planets they descended upon, but this was not Jonson's fate. Landing in a remote region of Caliban, he found himself encircled by wooded wilderness, hundreds of miles away from the nearest fortress. How Jonson survived those early years is a mystery. By rights, he should have perished within his first few minutes, for the crash of his incubator pod would have alerted the beasts that ruled those lands. Somehow, the child managed not just to survive on one of the deadliest planets in the galaxy, but to grow tall and strong there in only a short span of years. What it was like for him none can say, for Jonson never spoke of those times himself. All that can be said with certainty is that for a decade, the young Primarch survived on his own. It was in this savage state that the Primarch had his first encounter with other humans.

THE ORDER

The knights that Jonson encountered belonged to a group known simply as the Order. Famous for their code of honour and fearless skill in battle, the Order was unique amongst the knights of Caliban, for their members were selected on merit rather than by inheritance. Anyone, even lowborns, could join, and contingents of their selfless knights travelled the planet, giving aid to those in need. It was on one of their expeditions that a band from the Order came upon a wild man. Thinking him a beast, the knights were ready to enter battle when one of their number, Luther, halted his fellows, sensing that there was something more to the creature than was at first apparent. The knights returned to civilisation, taking with them the man born of the forest. Because of his appearance and the place of his discovery, the Order gave the wild man the name of Lion El'Jonson, which meant 'The Lion, the Son of the Forest'. They were amazed to see how easily Jonson adapted to the ways of humans, learning their language, traditions and sciences incredibly quickly. Yet of his past, he would not speak.

Within the fortress monastery of the Order, the Primarch was assimilated into society. There, he and Luther formed a close friendship, although they were quite different. Where Luther was charismatic, Jonson was taciturn. While Luther was rash and quick to change his mind, Jonson was a brilliant strategist, stubborn to a fault once he decided on a course of action. Despite their opposition on many things, the two men seemed to fill in the gaps in each other's personalities and they became an incomparable team.

In the following years, Jonson and Luther rose through the ranks of the Order. Their many exploits became legend – they hunted the most ferocious monsters of Caliban, fought famous duels against their mightiest rivals, and performed masterful feats of tactical genius on battlefields in the most far-flung locales. Their reputation, as well as that of the Order, rose as never before. As the Order grew in power, building many additional fortress monasteries, Jonson and Luther argued that now was the time for a crusade against the monsters that infested the forests, a war to cleanse the planet once and for all of their foul presence. It was the persuasive oratory skills of Luther that convinced the Grand Masters of the monasteries, along with most of the planet's nobles, to join the sweeping crusade. It was Jonson's supreme ability at organising the campaign, however, that ensured that, within a decade, the entire planet was cleared of the monstrous creatures that had once dominated its lands. A golden age dawned for the inhabitants of the once troubled planet.

In recognition of his triumph against the monsters, Lion El'Jonson was proclaimed the new Supreme Master of the Order, and of the entire planet of Caliban. Although Luther did not openly begrudge Jonson this honour, he would not have been human if he did not feel some twinge of jealousy, for had he not also played a part in the victory? Thus was struck the first spark that would, one day, lead to the schism that would tear the Dark Angels apart. But all that was in the future – for the present, the people of Caliban enjoyed a time of hitherto unheard of peace and prosperity.

THE EMPEROR REACHES CALIBAN

Unbeknownst to the people of Caliban, the Emperor had been waging his Great Crusade to reunite humanity. As the wave of conquests spread, scouts rediscovered long-isolated Caliban. Soon, the Emperor was reunited with another of his lost Primarchs, and the meeting was as filled with joy as a father finding a long lost son. Seeing what he had already accomplished on Caliban, the Emperor's first action was to give Lion El'Jonson control of the Dark Angels – a Legion of Space Marines created using Jonson's own gene-seed, one of the twenty Legions that the Emperor forged using genetic material from the Primarchs.

Lion El'Jonson recognised the opportunity to bring hope to Mankind across the galaxy. Caliban was made the home of the Dark Angels and the whole of the Order moved to join its ranks. Those knights still young enough had the Legion's gene-seed implanted to turn them into Space Marines. Those too old for this process underwent transformative surgery, and while they would never match the strength, speed or resilience of a true Space Marine, they could be counted amongst the elite warriors of the Imperium. The first to be brought into the legion in this manner was Luther, who remained Jonson's second-in-command.

THE GREAT CRUSADE

Jonson and the Dark Angels set out with the Emperor to continue the battle for humanity's dominance of the galaxy. After the first few campaigns, however, Luther was sent back to Caliban, where he was to supervise the induction of the next generation of recruits into the Legion. Despite the importance of Luther's new position, it was not one suited to his ambitious personality. To Luther, returning to Caliban felt more like a dismissal than a pivotal role.

THE SON OF THE FOREST

Ten seasons passed for the young Primarch who would become known as Lion El'Jonson. By this time he was full-grown, his genetically instilled powers accelerating his growth. Cut off from human contact, he could not speak, only roar, as he hunted, and was hunted in turn.

One day, this wild-thing, more lion than man, heard a strange new sound. Accustomed to the hunting calls of mutated creatures, this was unlike any he had heard before. It was the sound of human laughter. Overcome with curiosity, the Primarch was drawn to a hunting party in a clearing, laughing and talking over the slain body of a ferocious monster. Amazed, the feral man studied these strange beings – for they were much like himself. Forgetting his naturally learned caution, however, almost cost him his life.

One of the knights spied Jonson on the edge of the glade, but what he saw was not a man, but some form of wild beast stalking his party. Instinctively, the knight drew his weapon and loosed a volley of shots. Only the Primarch's lightning fast reactions saved him from death, but even so, several shells hit home. Reeling, the wild-man tried to escape, but was surrounded, for many of the hunting party were mounted upon great black steeds. His back pressed against a tree, Jonson growled at the knights, preparing to sell his life dearly.

Many wars were fought in the Great Crusade to drive out Orks, Eldar and worse. Many human-held planets refused to bow before the Emperor, for they had been long cut off from contact and were mistrustful. Some of these were honourable men, merely misguided; however, others were tyrants, greedy to retain their power. Worse, some had listened to whisperings from the Warp, succumbing to the will of Daemons and raising their war banners against all humanity. The Space Marine Legions fought an endless succession of foes, yet they were undismayed, for they were mighty and their commanders were invincible.

In this savage age, the Primarchs walked the worlds like living gods. There were cataclysmic battles and terrible massacres, but also noble deeds and a sense of hope. After the long darkness of the Age of Strife, Mankind once more had a bright future. All the Legions pushed themselves, but of the Primarchs, Horus was the Emperor's favourite. The Lord of Humanity had every reason to be proud of him, for Horus led his Legion to great victories, and he was noble and respected by all who served him. While Horus was first among the Primarchs, there were others of near equal renown: Jaghatai Khan of the White Scars, cunning master of lightning raids, Angel-winged Sanguinius, of the pure heart, Leman Russ of the Space Wolves, impetuous and bold. And of course, grim Lion El'Jonson, whose silence held deep wisdom; whose fury, once risen, was second to none.

During this time, no record of the Dark Angels' victories was kept, but it is known that Jonson won wide acclaim for his masterful tactics and the tenacity of his Legion. It infuriated Jonson's fraternal rival, Leman Russ, to admit that another Primarch could claim more triumphs than he. Yet there was one who achieved even greater military success than Jonson – Horus and his Luna Wolves Legion. For his feats, Horus was named Warmaster – chief of all the Imperium's armies, and Warlord over his brother Primarchs. Meanwhile, as Jonson's fame spread and reports of his great deeds reached the Legion's homeworld, Luther chafed in his duty, feeling robbed of his share of the glory. His role as planetary governor seemed to him more and more like an insult.

Then came the nightmare betrayal of the Horus Heresy, the civil war that threatened to destroy the newborn Imperium. Before he openly displayed his nature, Warmaster Horus ordered the most staunchly loyal Legions, the ones he knew he could not corrupt, to distant war zones. So were the Blood Angels, the Ultramarines and the Dark Angels unable to counter Horus' initial moves.

Many tales have emerged from those cataclysmic times, but none capture the panic that gripped the Imperium. Whole systems rebelled and it was difficult to discern friend from foe. Warp storms cut communications, and the last message to get through was a garbled message about trouble on Caliban. Upon finally hearing of the disasters taking place, Lion El'Jonson hurried his Legion back to Terra. Their journey was delayed by Warp storms, Daemon attacks and traps set by the traitorous Legions, for half of the Space Marine Legions had been persuaded by Horus to rebel. When, at last, they reached Terra's orbit, Jonson saw they were too late. Events had taken their terrible course. The forces of Chaos were defeated, but the Imperium was in ruins and the Emperor was mortally wounded.

THE FALL OF CALIBAN

In the aftermath of the Horus Heresy, the surviving loyalists rallied the reeling Imperium. The Dark Angels took a significant part in these battles, which later came to be called the Scouring. As they pursued the rebels, the Legion diverted to nearby Caliban, which had been enshrouded by Warp storms since Horus' betrayal. For Lion El'Jonson, one final act of treachery remained to be discovered.

As the Dark Angels fleet moved into orbit, they were met by a barrage of defence laser fire. Ships exploded, plummeting into the planet like monstrous comets. Although stunned by the sudden attack, Jonson's superhuman reactions allowed what remained of the fleet to disengage, withdrawing to safety. The betrayal Jonson unravelled shook him to his very core. Over the decades Luther had brooded, nurturing a seed of jealousy. His hatred had spread, poisoning those under his command and several generations of new recruits. His powerful oratory skills had twisted their hearts with an all-consuming hatred of the new Imperium. Like Horus, Luther had been corrupted; his pride had been all the opening the Dark Gods needed to make him their own.

The fury of Lion El'Jonson and the remaining loyal Dark Angels knew no bounds. They had fought across the galaxy, but had arrived too late to aid their Emperor. Still, they had thought the Dark Powers on the run, only to find their own homeworld, their own brethren, corrupted and turned against them. Even as the horrors of the situation sunk in, Jonson formulated a battle plan. It began with the massed guns of the fleet disabling Caliban's defence laser batteries and driving the rebel Dark Angels into the shelter of their force field-protected fortress monasteries.

Knowing that one surgical strike could end the conflict, Lion El'Jonson personally led an assault on the greatest monastery of the old Order. He knew that this was where he would find Luther – and so it was that the two former friends faced each other. Although the Primarch possessed immense power, the two opponents were equally matched, for Luther's abilities were enhanced by vast forces gifted to him by the Dark Gods. What followed was a fight of titanic proportions. As the two adversaries traded blows, shock waves shook the monastery, causing chunks of masonry to crash down around them. Outside, the guns of the Dark Angels fleet pounded the planet, reducing the other monasteries to miles-wide craters, angry magma spewing from the wounds gouged into the planet's crust. Caliban's surface began to crack under the bombardment, and the fury of the Dark Angels blinded them to the devastation they were wreaking.

As the planet broke apart, the battle between Jonson and Luther reached its climax. Already weakened by the long fight, Luther staggered, leaving an opening. But despite his rage, Lion El'Jonson could not bring himself to slay his former friend. As he hesitated, Luther unleashed a furious psychic attack that knocked Jonson to his knees and left him mortally wounded. As the dying Primarch struggled to stand, a veil was lifted from Luther's eyes and he realised the full extent of his deeds. His was a triple betrayal: of his friend, of the Dark Angels, and of the Emperor. The truth shattered his sanity and he slumped down beside the ailing Jonson, issuing a cry of pain and despair that echoed through the Warp.

Upon hearing that sound, the Chaos Gods realised that, once more, they had been denied. They howled in frustration, and across the galaxy psykers fell to their knees. So powerful was the cry that a rent appeared in the fabric of space and a Warp storm emerged to engulf what remained of Caliban. Those 'Fallen' Dark Angels who had served under Luther were sucked from the broken surface into the Warp and cast throughout time and space. The remains of Caliban, weakened by the bombardment, were ripped asunder, destroyed in a last apocalyptic explosion.

Only a single part of the planet survived the vortex that pulled the rest of the crumbling debris into the Warp. Protected by an ancient force field, the ruins of the fortress monastery and a massive hunk of the planet's bedrock still remained, held together and floating alone in the empty vacuum of space. The Dark Angels flew down to the surface of the remaining rock and gazed in horror at what was left of their once verdant home world. At the heart of the empty wasteland they found Luther, bloody, cringing and gibbering, but they were unable to extract anything coherent out of the shell of a man who had once been Jonson's closest friend.

Luther repeated the same words over and over again: the Primarch had been carried away by the Watchers in the Dark and one day he would return to forgive Luther for the terrible sins he had committed. Of the mighty Primarch, Lion El'Jonson, there was no sign.

THE LION AND THE WOLF

Perhaps the most famous rivalry in the Imperium is between the Dark Angels and the Space Wolves. It chafed the bombastic Space Wolf Primarch to see that Lion El'Jonson had more victories than he and matters came to a head on the world of Dulan, where the two Legions fought against the Tyrant Durath. After a personal insult, Russ swore he would cut Durath's head off and demanded that the Dark Angels stand down. Jonson, who had spent days laying meticulous plans, refused and launched his own attack. The Dark Angels swept into the citadel, and Jonson killed Durath. Caught flat-footed, Russ' sole contribution to the fight was to howl in frustration. After the battle, Russ struck Jonson a blow. Jonson rose to his feet and struck back. A space was cleared and the two Primarchs wrestled while their assembled men cheered. Each Primarch was matched in superhuman strength and speed – if Russ was slightly stronger, then Jonson was marginally quicker. Each knew every trick and feint, and the fight lasted a day and a night. Russ, quick to rage but also to mirth, saw the funny side of what had happened and began to laugh. For him, the fight was over; both men had taken each other's measure. Jonson, however, was silent; he was slow to anger and slow to forgive, and he saw Russ' first blow as treacherous. As Russ laughed, Jonson struck him unconscious. The prone form of Russ was carried from the fortress by his men, and now Jonson, in turn, considered honour satisfied. When Russ awoke, the Dark Angels were gone, leaving him to swear that he would have vengeance for Jonson's low blow. Thus began a feud that still endures, for to this day, when Space Wolves and Dark Angels meet, a champion from each Chapter is called upon to refight that ancient duel.

Dark Heritage

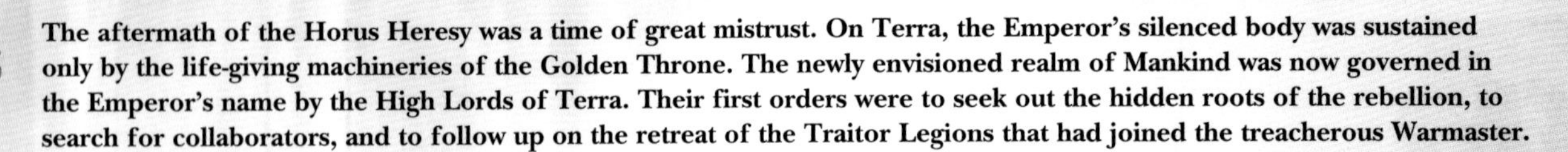

The aftermath of the Horus Heresy was a time of great mistrust. On Terra, the Emperor's silenced body was sustained only by the life-giving machineries of the Golden Throne. The newly envisioned realm of Mankind was now governed in the Emperor's name by the High Lords of Terra. Their first orders were to seek out the hidden roots of the rebellion, to search for collaborators, and to follow up on the retreat of the Traitor Legions that had joined the treacherous Warmaster.

All record and memory of the Traitor Legions was expunged from the Imperial archives and their homeworlds and bases of operations were attacked. All across the Imperium, a tangled web of suspicion hung over everything, misdoubts that were only made worse as further investigations revealed yet deeper corruption. Thus began the Age of the Imperium, an era steeped in paranoia, recriminations and vengeance. After all, if Horus – the right hand of the Emperor – could turn traitor, who might be next?

It was in this new age of fear and doubt that the remaining Dark Angels assembled to pay tribute to their lost Primarch. Internalising their grief, the Dark Angels pulled together, their Masters forming a plan of action. They were still the Sons of the Lion – tenacious warriors who, once stirred to action, were never short of zeal. In a way, the Dark Angels were born again, single-mindedly rededicating their lives to the service of the Imperium.

They decided the true story of treachery behind the destruction of Caliban must remain secret; no outsider must learn of the schism that split their Legion, or that any Dark Angels had ever turned to the Ruinous Powers. Should the truth be revealed, the Dark Angels would be labelled Excommunicate Traitoris and never given a chance to redeem themselves. The senior members of the Legion formed a secret conclave – an Inner Circle of the Legion's Masters. They created an overlapping system to watch over their own Brothers, and also themselves. Everyone must be scrutinised for signs of corruption. Thus started a spiral of mistrust and secrecy that continues to this day.

Such was the scale of the disaster that there could be no hiding it. Psykers across the galaxy had sensed the Warp storm, and the titanic flash of the tempest meeting the indomitable force field had blazed like a supernova. However, the Dark Angels had a systematic cover up of the truth in place, for each remaining battle-brother had taken stringent vows of unspeakable binding to never reveal what really took place on Caliban. Their story might not have held up under an intense inquiry, but it was a time of great upheaval in the Imperium and the retreating Traitor Legions were bolder near the Eye of Terror: the Night Lords, in particular, laid many ambushes that took a high toll on their Imperial pursuers. That a Warp storm had claimed the Dark Angels' homeworld, and so many of their brethren, was but another tragedy in a deluge of grim tidings.

Inquiries found the Dark Angels battered, grief-stricken and bereft of reinforcements, but there was little time for any succour, for war called. Across the galaxy, traitor strongholds remained and many rebellious planets had yet to be shown the error of their judgement, but most ominous of all was the rise of the xenos threat. So much of the Imperium's strength was siphoned off in the civil war, and countless planets found themselves at the mercy of a new wave of xenos attacks. Leaving only those necessary to oversee the work being done on the Rock, the Dark Angels split their remaining fleet in an attempt to answer the many distress calls that reached them.

In the Cadian sector they joined the Blood Angels, themselves still reeling from the loss of their Primarch Sanguinius. Together, like vengeful angels, they drove back traitors and Daemons alike. On Seption Prime, Dark Angels Terminator companies arrived just in time to provide a rearguard action, allowing the Ultramarines to extract their forces before the plague planet was destroyed by Exterminatus. All who fought alongside the Dark Angels lauded them as steadfast warriors, utterly dedicated to the destruction of the Emperor's enemies.

Upon their return to the Rock, the much-depleted Dark Angels found disturbing news. At the time of the Fall, the Dark Angels thought their traitorous brethren had all been destroyed, vanquished in the Warp storm that blossomed in the death throes of Caliban. The Fallen Dark Angels had been swept into the vortex of that horrific rent in the galaxy, but the fury of the Dark Gods had not slain them. The scryings of the Legion's Librarians searched long and hard for their missing Primarch and of him they could read no signs. They did, however, pick up traces of the Fallen and determined that the traitors yet lived, although what remained of their psychic signatures were widespread, and the connections were already fading out of mindsight.

The Masters of the Legion greeted this new shock with typical stoicism, despite the inner turmoil it created. On the one hand, they feared their nightmare would be revealed – that while the Fallen lived, knowledge of their Legion's treachery might be spread throughout the galaxy. On the other hand, the continued existence of the traitors offered hope, for if the renegades could be tracked down and forced to repent, then the sins of the Legion might be absolved, washed away in the blood of the Fallen. The Grand Masters of the nascent Inner Circle swore that so long as even one of the Fallen remained alive and unrepentant, the Dark Angels would be Unforgiven, cursed by their brothers to atone for all eternity. So began the secret mission that would prove the driving force behind the Dark Angels' actions for millennia to come.

The Rock

Following the destruction of Caliban, the Dark Angels made the Rock their new home. Never was there a gloomier sight, for although the Warp storm that scoured Caliban could not penetrate the ancient shields, they left an indelible mark. The force field over the fortress monastery held, but was rent with cracks. To this day, there exists a disturbance within the field's protective shell, as if part of that tempest still rages within. Great chain-lightnings arc across the artificial atmosphere that surrounds the craggy Rock, briefly outlining the ruins that crown the asteroid.

The Dark Angels explored the halls and dungeons they found beneath the fortress monastery. There, they claimed the hoard of machinery that had sat untouched since the little-understood Age of Technology. Many of the devices from that apex of human invention still worked, like the great shield generator itself, although their mechanisms were now unfathomable. Although the existent halls were large, a massive labour carved out deeper and deeper catacombs beneath the asteroid's bedrock, excavating room for an entire Legion. With the aid of the Tech-priests of Mars, docks were added, allowing for the entrance of spacecraft. Although it took centuries to complete, the Rock was also outfitted with Warp engines, allowing the Dark Angels' headquarters to travel across the galaxy. While the artisans did marvellous work, crafting halls full of clustered columns rising to arched vaults, and much-decorated ceremonial crypts to hold the Legion's sacred items, it was a grim place, full of echoes and cold stone.

Although only a fraction of what was once Caliban, the Rock is larger than even the heaviest class of starship, and it bears formidable firepower. The sheer sides of its mass are studded with gun turrets, lance batteries, torpedo tubes, observation blisters, and comm-relays. Its cavernous docking bays can accommodate many hundreds of smaller craft – including Thunderhawk gunships, Nephilim Jetfighters and escort frigates.

No effort was made to rebuild the ruined Tower of Angels atop the Rock, and even now it remains undisturbed and eerily silent, protected from the cold depths of space by the same force fields that shrouded it from the destruction of Caliban. Although attempts have been made to mask it, an unusual energy signature emanates outwards from the Rock, portending of some great power hidden within. Beneath the shattered ruins, many dark secrets lay cloistered from sight, and the deeper into the Rock's labyrinth of dungeons one goes, the closer one comes to the truth.

THE PATH TO REDEMPTION

Once the course of absolution was decided, the Dark Angels moved with speed and conviction. Lion El'Jonson had introduced the structure he had learned from the Order on Caliban, and now the remaining Dark Angels took that brotherhood a step further, becoming even more monastic in manner. The Lion's tenets of loyalty, discipline and self-efficiency were incorporated into everything the Legion did, and every move was now accompanied by prayers and rituals. Even as the Rock was outfitted to become, in essence, their new mobile homeworld, the Dark Angels were laying down the new rigours that would govern them.

That the Dark Angels were acting suspiciously and growing more insular was noted by many watchful eyes. At this time entire new divisions, such as the Inquisition, were developed with the sole purpose of seeking out and destroying internal corruption. Inspections following the destruction of Caliban judged the Dark Angels fit to continue. Some leeway for their new reclusive behaviour was granted due to the simultaneous loss of the Legion's Primarch and homeworld, but largely it was allowed because of the Dark Angels' ongoing and relentless heroics against the Imperium's foes. Regardless, they would continue to be closely monitored.

As the Legion had come from the gene-seed of the stalwart, if reticent, Lion El'Jonson, the Dark Angels had always been regarded as dedicated and serious-minded warriors. Like their primogenitor, they were slow to anger, but tenacious and all but unstoppable once roused. After the disappearance of their Primarch, it did not seem that strange for the remaining Dark Angels to withdraw further into their own brotherhood. If before they had been described as reserved, now they were, at best, taciturn: at worst, they were cold and austere. Behaviour that once would have been described as pensive was now more like a brooding silence. Yet there was one thing that had not changed – their campaigns continued to be well-planned and effective actions. If the Dark Angels were in some strange mourning, it in no way dampened their ability to bring battle to the enemies of the Imperium.

Many changes were happening within the Imperium during these darksome days. Although Horus had been defeated and his remaining Traitor Legions driven into the Eye of Terror, the High Lords of Terra and the remaining Primarchs still dreaded the resurgence of Chaos. They had all recoiled in horror at the full realisation of how insidious the betrayal had been, how far across the galaxy the roots of corruption had spread. Never again could the Imperium be subjected to such widespread rebellion; drastic measures had to be undertaken.

To avoid the threat of the Space Marine armies, Mankind's most elite warriors, falling under the influence of the enemy, the remaining Legions were sub-divided into a number of smaller Chapters. Before the Horus Heresy, a Space Marine Legion might count ten thousand or more warriors under a single command, but under the new structure each Chapter's size was limited to a thousand warriors.

The organisation, tactics and roles of these new 'Chapters' were defined in a hugely influential work known as the Codex Astartes. Roboute Guilliman, the Primarch of the Ultramarines, almost single-handedly undertook the work for the Codex Astartes. These proscriptions not only lessened the risks of a single traitor altering the course of the Imperium, but also allowed the limited number of Space Marines to be more flexible – spreading more widely across the galaxy to confront Mankind's many enemies.

Sensing vulnerability, the enemies of Mankind had taken advantage of the preoccupied and weakened Imperium, and had chosen that time to invade. Across thousands of planets over all four Segmentums, humanity was once again besieged. Guilliman needed multiple mobile fighting armies to send immediately to the far-flung frontiers where anarchy and xenos threatened to devour Mankind's tenuous hold.

The first act of creating smaller, more versatile Chapters out of the original Legions became known as the Second Founding, and those new Chapters were known as Successor Chapters. Although autonomous, Successor Chapters naturally claimed close ties to their originating Legion, and this proved especially true with the Dark Angels. It is unknown exactly how many were created, as some have since been destroyed and the records of that time have been lost.

The Dark Angels acquiesced to the order to split, as doing otherwise would raise suspicion at a time when they could ill afford any scrutiny. From their Legion, they sired the Angels of Absolution, the Angels of Redemption and the Angels of Vengeance, each new Chapter led by its own Grand Master. While showing all pretences of being independent, the Dark Angels' Successor Chapters regularly met, in clandestine fashion, to take their lead from the Grand Master of the Dark Angels Chapter – for although they had been divided, the Successor Chapters too had witnessed the Fall of Caliban, and thus remained part of the Unforgiven, carrying forth their secrets with them.

THE DARK ORACLE

Near the heart of the Rock resides a single cell. It is deep in the bowels of the asteroid, where only the Watchers in the Dark and the Supreme Grand Master are allowed to venture. There, past locked gates that are shielded with dozens of feet of adamantine plating, is an oubliette. Its walls are inscribed with the most potent runes of warding known to men, and they have been inscribed to keep creatures out, but also to keep something within. There, sustained in life for ten thousand years by a powerful stasis field, languishes the broken man who was once known as Luther.

Down the ages, the Supreme Grand Masters have had some success in using Luther as an oracle. Although his Warp-contaminated and deranged mind often wanders or attempts to deceive, during moments of lucidity the Luther-thing speaks of events that will be, or might be, or drops hints at what is hidden and where.

Since the Fall of Caliban, each Supreme Grand Master has, in turn, taken the long dark walk down to the heavily psi-warded cell. Each has tried to extract a confession from the arch-heretic, each has tried to penetrate the madness that clouds him; none have succeeded. The thing that was, and may still be, Luther has divulged many secrets – from the names and locations of members of the Fallen, to the whereabouts of relics from the Legion secreted in the underworks beneath the old fortress monastery. Mostly, however, all that can be gotten out of Luther are mad ravings – over and over again he repeats that he has no need of repentance or confession, for one day Lion El'Jonson will return and absolve him of his sins. He claims that day is near and that he can feel the Lion is already close at hand...

THE INNER CIRCLE

As the decades since the Fall of Caliban turned to centuries, the Inner Circle took shape. It grew from an ad-hoc conclave to a formal, if still furtive, organisation that spread through not just the Dark Angels, but their Successor Chapters as well. Recruitment planets were founded and new generations of Dark Angels were added, replacing the ranks of those lost in battle. The regimens and drills of the Chapter were strict, with special emphasis on brotherhood and loyalty. However, the Masters and elder warriors who led the instruction told the neophytes nothing of the sins of their forefathers. The truth of what occurred and knowledge of the Fallen was withheld, now known only to the increasingly small number of brethren who had survived it.

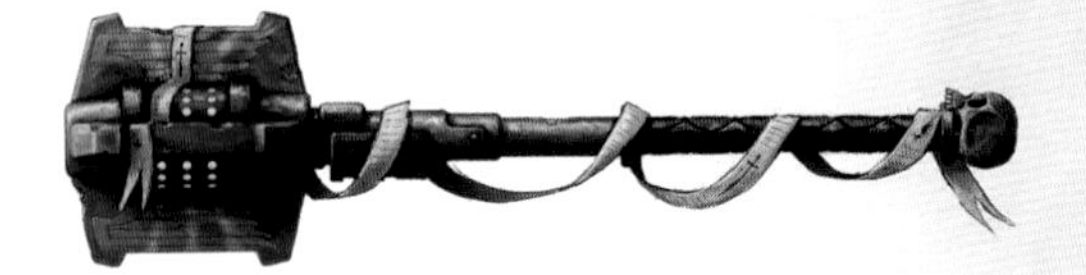

The Inner Circle hides its true face even from its own. Where many Space Marine Chapters openly celebrate their ancestors' achievements, the Dark Angels take great pains to tell their story one passage at a time. Much of the Dark Angels' teachings are couched in allegory and myth, the same essential truths told and retold, in one form after another. As veterans rise through the unseen levels of trust, more of the truth is gradually revealed to them by ranking members of the Inner Circle.

Only upon ascension to the 1st Company, known within the Dark Angels Chapter as the Deathwing, will a battle-brother begin to learn of the events that transpired at the dawn of the Age of the Imperium. This is the first ring of trust within the Inner Circle and those who are considered for membership are observed, unaware, by those within the hidden order and also by the diminutive Watchers in the Dark, the mysterious creatures that haunt the lower levels of the Rock. It is essential that only those who have proven their absolute loyalty to the Chapter time and time again are allowed to progress. Silent and hooded brothers lead any aspirants before the assembled Inner Circle for the great rituals of judgement, and those chosen are either elevated to the Deathwing, or disappear forever.

While a new member of the Inner Circle might suppose he has been told the entire tale, such is not the case. There remain circles within circles, levels within levels, with each step accompanied by its own rituals. Entering the 1st Company is only the beginning of the journey of truth. Rising through the intricate and convoluted ranks of the Inner Circle, a Dark Angel will learn more and more, each secret revealed as the Chapter's trust in him increases.

Given the planning skills inherited from their Primarch, the Dark Angels have instituted fail-safe systems that automate the passing on of knowledge should key members of the circle die without being able to properly reveal their secrets. There are some revelations that remain known only to those who gain ascension to the rank of Supreme Grand Master, the Chapter Master of the Dark Angels. And yet, there are still secrets to which even he is not privy.

The Hammer of Angels

With a bow to the statues that flanked the chamber, Brother Valefor, Librarian of the Dark Angels, approached the command altar of the strike cruiser, Sword of Absolution. *At his approach, a cluster of Watchers in the Dark scattered into the shadows, leaving only Belial poring over the maps and holo-displays.*

'Greetings, Grand Master Belial. I bring word from the clerestory dome; swift action may be required. The astropathic choir has picked up a distress call – a colony on Verdis Prime is under xenos attack and requests immediate aid. I also sense that our quarry may have landed there,' said Brother Valefor. 'Perhaps he hopes to escape us in the confusion of battle, or even make truck with the xenos.'

By flickering torchlight, Master Belial examined the datascroll. With a wave of his hand, Valefor was dismissed. When the Librarian had left, the room's darkest shadow stepped forwards, revealing the hooded figure of Interrogator-Chaplain Asmodai.

'We can ill-afford to deviate from our mission, Brother Belial,' hissed Asmodai from behind his skull-mask. 'We must find the one once known as Brother Orias. The colonists will serve only to distract us.'

'There is no need to remind me of our mission, Brother Asmodai,' replied Belial, his face stern. 'It is not our sole duty, however; leave the battle plan to me, and I will leave the interrogations to you.'

On Verdis Prime, the Imperial mining colony had retreated to their last compound. They could not comply with the Eldar ultimatum to evacuate; their transport was not due back in-system for years, and they had no craft capable of escaping orbit. Their only chance was that their distress call reached someone, but it was a desperate hope. Consolidating around their largest hab-base, the miners awaited the merciless xenos. They did not have to wait long: as the moon reached its zenith, bathing Verdis Prime in green light, graceful figures were revealed on the surrounding ridges and the gliding forms of sleek grav-tanks closed upon the miners like predators cruising towards their prey.

It was at that moment that the Dark Angels arrived upon the field of battle. The roar of jet engines swept overhead as a Thunderhawk sped towards the front lines, and all around the perimeter of the base, the screaming descent of Drop Pods culminated in resounding thuds as the transports hit home. With cool precision, the Space Marines disembarked and formed a circle about the hab-base; instantly, the air resounded to the sound of bolter-fire. Explosions lit the distant hills, where the silhouettes of xenos infantry scattered to cover as their vehicles burned. Beams of lance-light stabbed down from the hills, blasting chunks out of the ferrocrete buildings and clanging off the reinforced holding silos. The terrified miners peered from vision slits, barely able to identify their saviours.

Black-armoured Ravenwing bikers zoomed from cover behind the cluster of buildings, their guns stitching patterns of death before them. Land Speeders streaked overhead, their weapons firing salvos at distant targets. In response, the xenos weapons raged, but the fire was heavier this time – not just infantry and tanks as before, but something larger and more powerful. From the ridgeline, the Eldar war machine rained fire down onto the Space Marines. It seemed akin to a Titan, yet more graceful than any Imperial machine.

On the distant ridgelines, the telltale flash of energy signatures marked teleporting Terminators, their pale armour stark in the predawn darkness. The newcomers arrived with guns blazing, and though their storm bolter fire had little effect, the irresistible blue streak of a plasma blast struck home again and again, at last bringing the giant down onto one knee. The heavily clad Terminators strode forwards, advancing behind the interlocked shields of their lead squad. Against such an assault, the xenos could not stand. As dawn broke over the horizon, the battle was won, and the miners emerged into the dazzling daylight to a scene of desolation.

The men gazed in amazement at the harbingers of their salvation. But the Dark Angels were not finished – gathering the colonists together, the superhuman warriors began a scrupulous inspection of the populace. Each miner in turn felt the glaring eyes of the hooded Space Marines penetrating their very souls, and many felt their so-called saviours seemed no more human than the Eldar they had so mercilessly destroyed. At last, a single man was taken; a newcomer who was led away for questioning. Upon the arrest of this unfortunate, the Dark Angels departed with no word of explanation. One alone turned to face the men – a black-armoured figure with a sinister skull-mask.

'Praise be to the Emperor,' he growled, not turning away until every citizen had repeated the proclamation. It was with unrestrained relief that the miners watched the last Thunderhawk blast off from Verdis Prime, leaving the colonists to count the cost of the battle alone.

Chapter Organisation

When the Space Marine Legions were broken down into smaller Chapters, the Dark Angels were one of the few that did not strictly follow the organisation laid out in the Codex Astartes. Some, such as the Space Wolves, were bold in their disregard, but the Dark Angels are subtler in their transgressions, and an outside observer might be hard-pressed to spot the differences.

Rule over the Dark Angels falls to the Supreme Grand Master and his council of Grand Masters. This is sometimes referred to as the Inner Circle – an old Caliban name that has secretive meanings unknown to all but the highest ranking officers of the Unforgiven Chapters. Members of the Inner Circle include the Chapter's Librarians, the Interrogator-Chaplains, and a small number of Company Masters, including the leaders of the 1st and 2nd Companies. Some Company Masters carry titles from the Codex Astartes, such as Master of the Fleet or of the Arsenal, while others are unique to the Dark Angels, such as Master of the Watchers, or Keeper of the Unseen Ritual.

Ten companies of Space Marines make up the bulk of the Dark Angels Chapter. Although each company can, and does, fight as a separate unit, their flexible nature and the multitude of war zones in which they fight often means that squads from different companies are assembled ad hoc in order to execute a mission. Each company is led by a Master, and he is often attended by a Command Squad. Many companies are also assigned a Chaplain, a warrior-priest who presides over spiritual wellbeing and stirs battle fury. Of the ten companies of the Dark Angels Chapter, the first two – the Deathwing and Ravenwing – are unique and do not follow standard Codex organisation. Rumours persist that they do not conform to the standard company complement. Contingents from both companies are found as part of most Dark Angels strike forces.

THE DEATHWING

The 1st Company is called the Deathwing and consists entirely of veteran troops, with an additional upper echelon of Masters-in-training known as Deathwing Knights. Their many triumphs have made the company famous across the galaxy. All members of the Deathwing fight in Terminator armour and are never fielded in power armour, as is the case with other Chapter's 1st Companies. The Deathwing use their own distinctive heraldry, and their armour is bone white, not the dark green colour used by the rest of the Chapter.

THE RAVENWING

The 2nd Company of the Dark Angels is known as the Ravenwing and it is, perhaps, even more unusual in its composition that the Deathwing. They are a highly specialised mobile formation used for scouting and lightning-fast strikes, where speed is more of a premium than firepower. To this end, every single Space Marine in this company is mounted on a bike or Land Speeder, or flies an atmospheric fighter. Many of the vehicle designs are unique to the Dark Angels and their Successor Chapters. These squads are organised into units called Attack or Support squadrons, and their vehicles, like their power armour, are an ominous black.

THE COMPANIES

The remainder of the Chapter is organised along standard Codex lines. The 3rd, 4th, and 5th Companies are battle companies – the backbone of the Chapter's fighting ability and the core of any prolonged campaign. In large battles, these formations generally form the centre and will be counted upon to bear the brunt of the fighting.

The 6th and 7th Companies are tactical companies, each consisting entirely of Tactical squads. These act as a reserve which may be used to bolster the front line, launch diversionary attacks or stem enemy flanking moves.

The 8th Company consists of Assault squads, typically equipped with jump packs. When deployed en masse, this company is used to storm an enemy – quickly closing with a foe and engaging in close ranged or hand-to-hand combat.

The 9th Company consists solely of Devastator squads. It is the most powerfully armed company in the Chapter, and is used to bolster defence points and provide long-ranged fire support.

The 10th Company consists of Scout squads; youths who have been partially transformed into Space Marines. This Company is the future of the Chapter and has no formal size as the rate of recruitment operates under a wide number of variables. Those Scout squads nearest to completing their training are assigned to strike forces. It is almost unheard of for the 10th Company to fight as a single unit.

COMPANY SUPPORT

All of the companies, with the exception of the Deathwing, the Ravenwing and the 10th Company, maintain Rhino and Razorback transports for each of their squads and masters. More vehicles are held centrally by the armoury, while Drop Pods are held by the fleet. The Deathwing has designated Land Raiders, and more are held in the armoury for use as requested by a Company Master. Although maintained by the armoury, it is customary for Dreadnoughts to remain a part of the company in which the warrior served before being interred. When not active, Dreadnoughts can be found powered down in the Halls of Silence.

The Dark Angels Chapter includes a large number of support staff, the great majority of which are human serfs, though there are a few Space Marines amongst their number. Most of these are non-combatants of advanced years, tasked with leading the day-to-day administration of the Chapter, such as the Victuallers, or the Master of Recruits. A particularly vital branch of the Chapter's support staff is that within the armoury. These include the Chapter's Techmarines, and their vast number of mono-task Servitors that perform mundane work and maintenance.

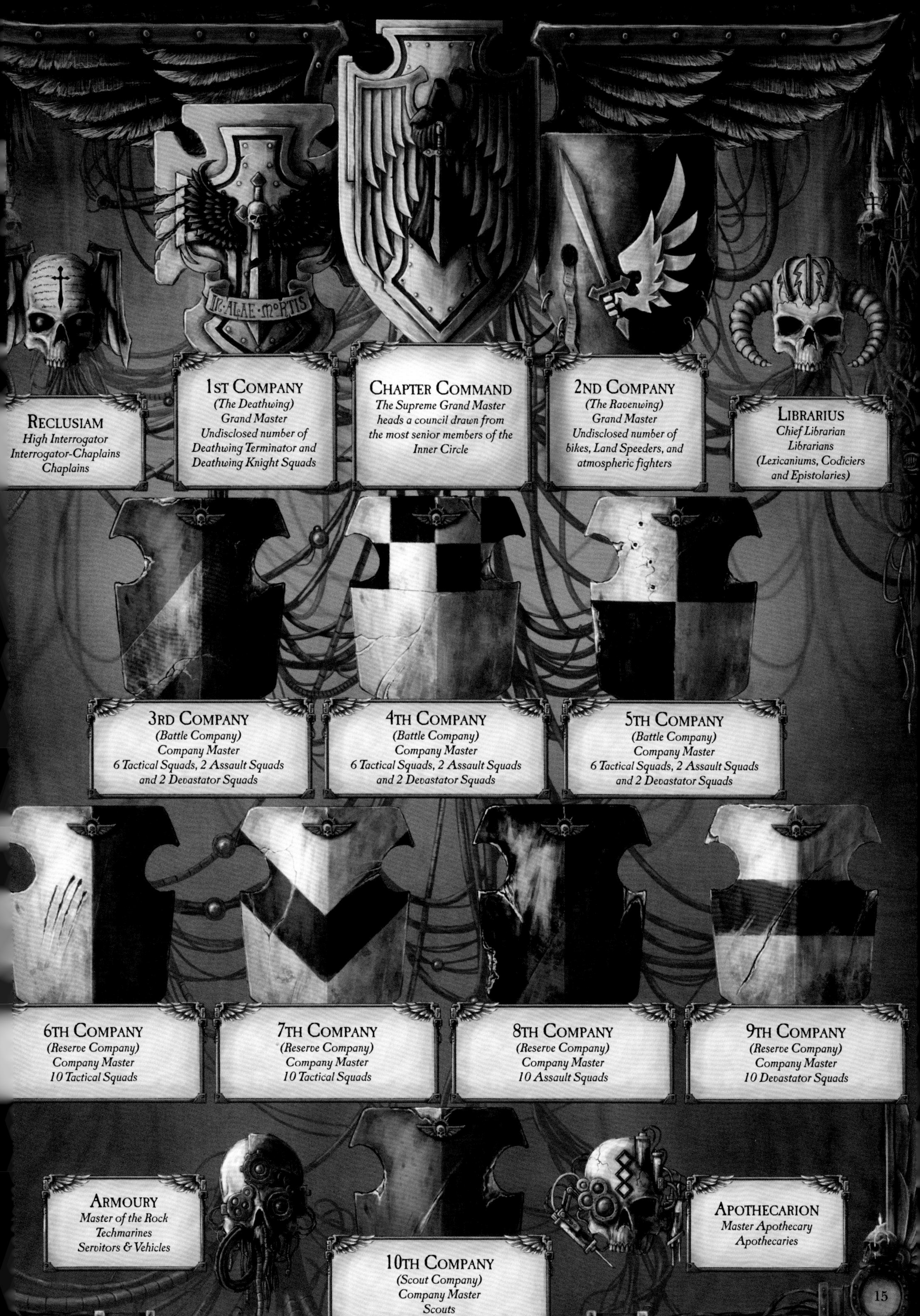
IN·ALAE·MORTIS
RECLUSIAM
High Interrogator
Interrogator-Chaplains
Chaplains
1ST COMPANY
(The Deathwing)
Grand Master
Undisclosed number of
Deathwing Terminator and
Deathwing Knight Squads
CHAPTER COMMAND
The Supreme Grand Master
heads a council drawn from
the most senior members of the
Inner Circle
2ND COMPANY
(The Ravenwing)
Grand Master
Undisclosed number of
bikes, Land Speeders, and
atmospheric fighters
LIBRARIUS
Chief Librarian
Librarians
(Lexicaniums, Codiciers
and Epistolaries)
3RD COMPANY
(Battle Company)
Company Master
6 Tactical Squads, 2 Assault Squads
and 2 Devastator Squads
4TH COMPANY
(Battle Company)
Company Master
6 Tactical Squads, 2 Assault Squads
and 2 Devastator Squads
5TH COMPANY
(Battle Company)
Company Master
6 Tactical Squads, 2 Assault Squads
and 2 Devastator Squads
6TH COMPANY
(Reserve Company)
Company Master
10 Tactical Squads
7TH COMPANY
(Reserve Company)
Company Master
10 Tactical Squads
8TH COMPANY
(Reserve Company)
Company Master
10 Assault Squads
9TH COMPANY
(Reserve Company)
Company Master
10 Devastator Squads
ARMOURY
Master of the Rock
Techmarines
Servitors & Vehicles
10TH COMPANY
(Scout Company)
Company Master
Scouts
APOTHECARION
Master Apothecary
Apothecaries

Dark Angels Successor Chapters

When the Space Marine Legions split into Chapters after the Horus Heresy, the Dark Angels Legion sired at least three new Chapters, but more are rumoured to exist. Although frequently passed over in subsequent Space Marine foundings, the Dark Angels have periodically been requested to give gene-seed to found new Chapters.

The Dark Angels Successor Chapters collectively call themselves the Unforgiven, for their own Inner Circles are aware of the ancient Legion's history, and they too seek to absolve themselves of the ancient failure. Each of the Unforgiven Chapters follows the Dark Angels' pattern of organisation, including their own corresponding levels of trust. Most have formations similar to the Deathwing and Ravenwing companies, although they are not named as such.

The Unforgiven coordinate their actions, and it is not unknown for the Supreme Grand Masters of all the Chapters to gather for summit meetings on the Rock. Although duty-bound to run their formations independently, it is strongly suspected by some within the Imperium that the Dark Angels' Successor Chapters show too much deference to the Supreme Grand Master of their originating Chapter. It is, at least partially, this rumour of 'Legion-building' that often persuades the High Lords of Terra to overlook the Dark Angels' gene-seed when seeking to create further Foundings.

THE ANGELS OF VENGEANCE

The deeds of the Angels of Vengeance are even less well known than those of the other Unforgiven Chapters, for they shun fame and laurels, instead concentrating on their duties to the exclusion of all else. They are a grim and dour organisation, with all of their companies wearing armour of jet black. This is a tribute to the panoply won by the original Dark Angels Legion, when they first set out from Terra on the Great Crusade.

The Angels of Vengeance embody one particular aspect of the Dark Angels' character above all others – a stubborn devotion to their cause bordering on the single-minded. The Chapter is wont to become embroiled in battles other forces would have little hope of winning, and emerging – bloody and battered – but victorious. The Angels of Vengeance are known to have suffered severe losses on several occasions; the result of their absolute refusal to retreat and their willingness to accept high casualties. The Chapter's future has been put in jeopardy more than once, beginning with their depletion in the Forgotten Wars. More recently, in the aftermath of the Siege of San Apolis, their losses were so extreme that the Chapter was forced to spend almost a century rebuilding before it could do battle once more.

Those who have observed the Angels of Vengeance have noted that they are unrelenting in their persecution of the foes of the Imperium. There is little hope of corralling their zeal against xenos, but that pales in comparison to their loathing of traitors, particularly any deemed to have even a connection to the Chaos Space Marines.

THE ANGELS OF REDEMPTION

Nothing can dissuade the Angels of Redemption from their mission to hunt down the Fallen, and it has been noted that the Chapter has, on occasion, withdrawn from a campaign in order to pursue their own undisclosed ends. It was at the height of the Defence of Gaitlinghive that the Angels of Redemption redeployed at the moment of the Orks' final assault, leaving seven brigades of Gaitlinghive militia to face an Orkish horde three million strong. The Angels of Redemption were never called to account for this act, as there were no survivors to press any form of inquiry. The Angels themselves embarked upon a hunt that led them to capture a Fallen Dark Angel – a victory, to them, worth the lives of the Gaitlinghive militia, and the population they fought to protect.

Perhaps due to this incident, and other similar events, Imperial forces have actually declined the aid of the Angels of Redemption. The consequences of their reputation have yet to emerge, but could range from Inquisitorial censure to outright excommunication, depending upon the Chapter's observed actions in coming years.

THE CONSECRATORS

The Consecrators Chapter is a mystery. No record of their existence is to be found prior to the third century of the 40th Millennium. The Chapter's first appearance is in the works of the field notary Corwen Quilp, in his account of the Second Kuppukin Schism.

At the height of this terrible war, loyalist forces were surrounded by the foe when the entire Consecrators Chapter deployed in their support. Though never answering friendly transmissions, the Consecrators launched an immediate attack upon the enemy and, within six hours, the Consecrators had wiped out the schismatists' entire high command structure, breaking the back of the rebellion, and essentially winning the war.

Their task complete, the Chapter withdrew, not to be seen for another three decades, when its 4th Company fought alongside the Dark Angels at the Arrulas Intervention. Though his descriptions are vague, Quilp is very specific on one element of the Consecrators' appearance – he noted that the brethren bore all manner of holy relics, and used the most ancient patterns of armour, weaponry and vehicles. It was as if, the field notary commented, the Consecrators had inherited the most revered arms of the Dark Angels Legion, preserving them lovingly, and bearing them down the ages against the foes of the Lion.

GUARDIANS OF THE COVENANT

It is not known from what founding the Guardians of the Covenant came, only that they too are part of the Unforgiven. Their adopted home world, Mortikah VII, lies near the western rim of the Imperium, and their mountain-top fortress monastery takes the form of a mighty cathedral, its spire piercing the clouds.

The Guardians of the Covenant have fought most of their battles within Segmentum Pacificus. They are known to have spearheaded a number of crusades into the Halo Stars and the Veiled Region. The Guardians of the Covenant gained special honours for their deeds during the Lelith Incursion, when they saved an entire sub-sector from a particularly appalling brand of xenos subjugation.

The Chapter is known for its exceptionally monastic character. True warrior-monks of the Emperor, they are assiduous in studying the teachings of the Emperor and of their Primarch. Their banners, armour and the flanks of their vehicles are covered in spidery, hand-written and illuminated text extracted from the pages of the Codex Astartes, the Requiem Angelis and many other tomes held sacred by the Space Marines.

THE DISCIPLES OF CALIBAN

The Founding of the Disciples of Caliban is shrouded in controversy. It is believed that Dark Angels Chapter Master Anaziel made a strong request of the High Lords of Terra for a Chapter to be raised late in the 37th Millennium. Much debate followed, for it is highly unusual for a Chapter Master to make such a request, and the reasons given by the Dark Angels for their petition were never shared, although it was eventually granted and the Disciples of Caliban created. Some have suggested that Anaziel must have had some sort of leverage over at least one of the High Lords of Terra for such a thing to have been achieved.

Their Founding gene-seed was of the highest pedigree held by the Dark Angels at the time, and scrutinised to a standard far beyond even that required by the Adeptus Terra. To this day, the purity of the Chapter's gene-seed is constantly monitored for the slightest sign of corruption or degradation, and it has the most exacting standards of recruitment of any of the Unforgiven. There have been whispers that Anaziel had the Disciples of Caliban created for a specific purpose, often rumoured amongst the other Unforgiven to be for the single-minded pursuit and capture of the renegade known as Cypher.

The Disciples of Caliban are a fleet-based Chapter, which has greatly aided the rapidity with which they can traverse the Imperium. Their flagship houses great reliquaries celebrating the success of their forebears. Each company has several Relic Bearers who carry the Chapter's most sacred artefacts to war to inspire the brethren. The most precious of these relics is the *Lionus Censum*, an immense scroll that details the names and deeds of the Chapter's most decorated battle-brothers.

'Fortune favours the faithful.'

THE ANGELS OF ABSOLUTION

The Angels of Absolution have been sighted throughout the known galaxy, most often seen fighting alongside the Dark Angels Chapter. The two Chapters often launch joint operations, such as the crusade against the Ork Empire of Charadon, the Battle at Archangel VII or the bloody suppression of the Rasputin uprisings.

In doctrine and temperament, the Angels of Absolution are very close to the Dark Angels. The two Chapters' teachings are largely consistent – the only divergence lies in the emphasis placed on the Chapter's guilt concerning the Fallen. Though it is a subtle distinction, the Angels of Absolution consider their own sins expunged by the actions of their forefathers in the Fall of Caliban. Though the Angels of Absolution fear no spiritual damnation from the Fall, they still consider themselves responsible for meting out the punishment upon the traitors.

Currently, the Angels of Absolution are wholly committed to stopping the Thirteenth Black Crusade, and all ten companies are deployed in some fashion on those battlefields around the Eye of Terror. They have reported back to the Rock the confirmed presence of several members of the Fallen amongst the traitorous forces.

The Hunt for the Fallen

That the Fallen exist is an anathema to the Dark Angels of the Inner Circle. That those who turned upon the Lion and caused his demise are still alive is an affront to the Space Marines that were made in his image, a stain on their honour. For the Unforgiven to gain redemption, the betrayers must be hunted down and made to repent.

During the final destruction of Caliban, the Fallen were subsumed within the swirling vortex and so entered the Warp for a period. The effects of that immersion are not fully known, as time and physical laws do not apply in that realm of utter Chaos. At least some of the Fallen were quickly cast back into realspace, scattered across the vast spread of the galaxy. Psychic readings of their positions were briefly ascertained by Dark Angels Librarians. Since that time, many thousands of years ago, the hunt for the Fallen continues, a constant and obsessive quest that the Inner Circle can never relinquish.

CYPHER

Of all the Fallen, none is as hated or feared as the enigmatic and deeply sinister individual known as Cypher. He appears as if from nowhere, bringing death and destruction with him, and then vanishes as abruptly as he arrived. Cypher's continued existence bears testimony to his supernatural ability to escape capture – the Dark Angels have had him surrounded many times, only to find he has, once again, eluded them. It is as if Cypher is personally watched over by dark forces that whisk him away when pursuers close upon him. Some of the Masters within the Dark Angels claim that Cypher is under the protection of some higher power and that he represents the Fallen Angels' only chance of redemption.

His features shrouded by a deep hooded cowl, Cypher rarely speaks, and his real name is unknown. The occasional glimpse of the dark green power armour beneath his long robes means – even to those outside of the Inner Circle – that there can be no doubt that Cypher is in some way connected to the Dark Angels.

It has been suggested that Cypher's seemingly random appearances hide a pattern that has simply not been discerned yet; there is a theory that he moves slowly across the galaxy towards Terra and the Emperor himself. Many have pointed to the fact that Cypher carries a sword which he never draws in combat, and that this could be the fabled Lion Sword, the blade once wielded by Lion El'Jonson himself and thought lost forever with his disappearance.

Whatever the truth about Cypher, it is certainly the case that when he appears in a place for any amount of time, he seems to attract other Fallen. Because of this, the members of the Inner Circle seek Cypher more than any other. They would perform almost any act, no matter how vile, in order to capture or kill him.

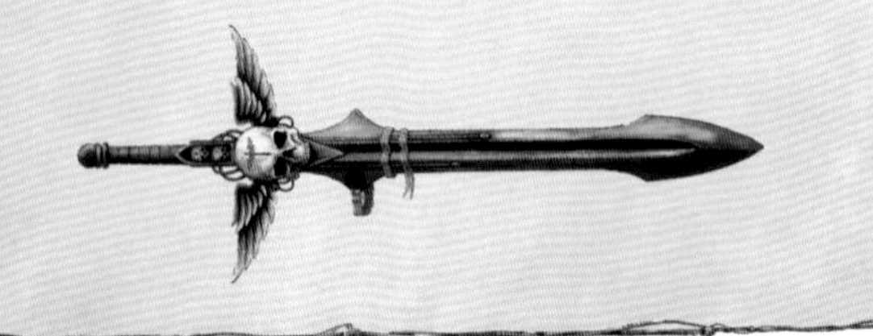

THE FALLEN

Although the Fallen Dark Angels chose the Ruinous Powers over their brethren, not all have succumbed to the power of Chaos to the same degree. Some of the Fallen have embraced the power of the Dark Gods, becoming true Chaos Space Marines. These Fallen do not belong to a Chapter or Legion of their own, but instead can be found operating together in small bands, or as leaders of some piratical cause. Each of the Fallen is a Space Marine possessed of Warp-aided powers. This, combined with the experience gained from their extended lifespans, makes the Fallen villains the likes of which are rarely seen in the 41st Millennium. They are towering giants amongst men, made at the dawning of the Imperium. The blood of their Primarch still runs in them – though it has been forever tainted. Some Fallen control armies of cultists; others have risen to become rulers of planetary empires, or have gathered bands of Chaos Space Marines beneath their banner in order to sow death and misery across whole sectors of the Imperium.

The Ruinous Powers are known to play cruel tricks. On occasion, a Fallen has appeared upon a world having just, to his frame of reference, been plucked from the disintegrating surface of Caliban. That thousands of intervening years have passed are, to him, just the blinking of an eye within the abyss of insanity that is the Warp. Driven wild with rage, such individuals launch themselves upon the hapless servants of the Imperium, becoming a terrible force of vengeance and raving aloud those secrets the Inner Circle have worked so long to keep silent.

Some of the Fallen have realised that their actions on Caliban were wrong. Disgusted by their weakness in the face of the corrupting influence of the Chaos Gods, and unable to reconcile themselves with their former order, they lead a forlorn, hunted existence. Many become mercenaries or rogue traders, roaming the edges of the galaxy as masterless men. Some attempt to atone for their sins, integrating themselves into human societies to work towards a noble cause – perhaps leading one of the uncounted outlying communities that slip through the cracks of the monolithic Imperium of Mankind.

The Dark Angels can go for years, even decades, without finding any rumours or clues that might lead to the capture of a Fallen. When they do, however, and they launch a successful mission, any captured Fallen are taken back to the Rock. Deep inside its dungeons, Interrogator-Chaplains attempt to make the Fallen repent. Occasionally they do, and for their pains, they die quickly. More often than not, however, the captured Fallen refuses and suffers a long, drawn-out and agonising death at the hands of those who would save his soul.

THE DEATHWING

On battlefields across the galaxy, the 1st Company of the Dark Angels, better known as the Deathwing, have earned their reputation as one of the most elite fighting forces within the Imperium. Made up entirely of the most proven and veteran warriors, every member of the company fights clad in Terminator armour. Each of the bulky suits is a venerable and nigh-impenetrable relic from a previous age, and the secrets of their making are either forgotten or so rare and hoarded that they are as good as lost.

The Deathwing is an assault force that is able to march, steady and intractable, into the very mouths of the heaviest of enemy guns. They are death-bringers that can teleport straight into the centre of battle, ripping out the heart of their foe. However, the Deathwing are more than just a heavily armed and armoured company of veteran Space Marines – the Deathwing is the clenched, mailed fist of the Inner Circle.

Only upon entering the Deathwing will a Dark Angel hear the story of Luther's betrayal, and that many of those that followed Luther are still alive. After absorbing this new knowledge, the newly joined Deathwing member is forever altered. He cannot help but feel the same abyssal feelings of betrayal and condemnation that his forefathers felt, for the blood of the original Dark Angels still runs through the veins of these latter-day Sons of the Lion. The new and mind-shattering understanding will unlock many feelings – an epiphany that suddenly explains many traditions and Chapter legends, unleashing the same inward rage and relentless abhorrence that the loyal members of the First Legion felt as they confronted the Fallen so long ago.

The Deathwing know that to eradicate the stain that covers more than 10,000 years of history, they must capture every one of the Fallen. This is a dangerous proposition, as they are formidable foes, apt to be surrounded by a cadre of bodyguards. If at all possible, the Deathwing attempt to catch suspected Fallen alive, turning them over to the Interrogator-Chaplains so that they might admit their sins and repent. The Fallen, even those who have tried to atone for their historic evils, will do their utmost to avoid this fate – making them fight with a hellish desperation.

Even within the Deathwing, there are multiple circles of trust, with older, more experienced warriors ensnared ever deeper into the spiderweb of secrets. The most veteran Deathwing warriors are given the title of Deathwing Knights, the uppermost level of the order before being named a Master. They become the ultimate upholders of ancient Chapter traditions and the most skilled fighting unit of the Dark Angels. In battle, the Deathwing Knights are fell-handed foes, Terminators armed with storm shields, wielding ancient weapons specially forged for vengeance. Few foes dare to stand before them – none do so for long.

APOCRYPHAL TALES

Dark Angels Terminators originally wore black armour, but it was painted bone white in honour of a battle fought long ago. Legends state that a band of Deathwing returned to the recruiting world of their birth only to find their people enslaved to Genestealer invaders. The brethren repainted their armour, symbolising that they were dead men walking, ghosts setting out on a death-quest. Fighting hordes of Genestealers, the brethren penetrated the alien lair, where they slew the hulking Broodlord that had long terrorised the galaxy. The battle claimed many of the Terminators' lives, but ultimately the world was freed.

Since that day, the Deathwing have kept their armour bone white, in remembrance of the sacrifice of their predecessors. The tale, known as the 'Battle of Two Heads Talking', after the famed Librarian who led the Terminators, is told by a hooded Sergeant to every Dark Angels Scout upon his elevation to battle-brother. Other oft-repeated tales in Dark Angels' lore are the 'Fall of the House of Pervigilium', 'The Scouring of the Space Hulk Place of Fears*', the 'Vengeance of Beleaguerest', 'the Lion and the Snake of Caliban' and 'Whisper in the Gloom'.*

All such Dark Angels legends are told at specific points in a brother's progress through the Chapter's ranks. Some tell of heroes returned from war to find their brothers corrupted, others speak of self-sacrifice or the refusal to accept surrender. No few touch upon those seeking redemption from dishonourable deeds. Such tales instill in every Dark Angel a zealous drive to right wrongs and seek out enemies, no matter where they might hide.

'By the way of their death we shall know them.'

'Forgiveness is a sign of weakness.'

THE RAVENWING

The Ravenwing, 2nd Company of the Dark Angels Chapter, is even more unusual than the Deathwing. Clad not in the usual green panoply of their Dark Angels brothers, but in grim, black armour, the Ravenwing formation is built for speed. The majority of the Space Marines in the company are deployed to battle on bikes, with the remainder piloting some form of Land Speeder or fighter aircraft.

The Ravenwing are ideal for fast assault missions, and they often perform as an outriding reconnaissance force, communicating back to the rest of the Chapter in order to coordinate an attack plan. Their originating function, however, is something altogether more sinister in nature. Although it is known only by the company's highest ranked officers – the Company Master and his Black Knight veteran squads – the Ravenwing's primary role is to hunt down and capture the Fallen. They are the relentless black-clad huntsmen that ride ahead of the rest of the Dark Angels, cutting out those who are targeted for capture.

Detached Ravenwing Land Speeders range far and wide across a battlefield, seeking the telltale signs passed down to them by the Inner Circle. When their quarry is marked, the Ravenwing is quick to switch from probing mode to a full-fledged assault. Formations on bikes roar forwards at breakneck speed, jinking to avoid incoming fire. Overhead, sleek atmospheric fighters keep the skies clear of enemy aircraft, while Land Speeders glide around the flanks to pour in supporting firepower. The bikers might race straight into the foe, using chainswords to slay those not crushed by the impact, or they might split off at the last minute, encircling the enemy to ensure that none can escape. They can also alert the Deathwing, who then arrive by teleportation to coordinates locked in by homers in the Ravenwing bikes. Face to face with the heavy firepower and close assault capabilities of the matchless Terminator squads, few enemies can resist for long.

Dark Angels are assigned to the Ravenwing for their ability to fight at breakneck speeds on fast attack vehicles; but they must also be possessed of the firmest conviction. They operate independently and far ahead of the rest of the army, and by necessity come into contact with heretics. Those they seek to capture are the worst kind of traitors, liars capable of spouting anything to undermine their captors' resolve. For this reason, the Ravenwing are trained to be deaf to their captives' lies and they are ministered to by Chaplains and monitored more closely than the rest of the Chapter, always checked for any sign of spiritual turmoil brought on by contact with such malignance.

NO COMBINATION MORE DEADLY

There is no underestimating the hard-hitting shock value the Deathwing and Ravenwing Companies bring to battle. While each is trained to perform a specific role – to seek out and destroy the Fallen – the formations have proven integral to all the Chapter's missions, regardless of foe. Whether deploying for a surgical, rapid strike or delivering a hammerblow assault, most Dark Angels forces include elements from both the Ravenwing and Deathwing.

A Master, or other strike force leader, will often leave his Deathwing allocations in reserve, as their Terminator suits are designed to be teleported into battle so that they arrive when and where they are most needed. In this way, the Deathwing can be used aggressively to land the killing blow, or can be called upon to block enemy advances, allowing the rest of the Dark Angels to regroup. The Deathwing, and especially Deathwing Knights, are often used to combat the most lethal of the enemy's troops.

The Ravenwing are the most tactically versatile formation in the Dark Angels, and Masters use 2nd Company allocations in all manner of battlefield roles. Most often, the bikes and Land Speeders are deployed as far-ranging reconnaissance or fast, flanking attackers. Ravenwing Attack Squadrons are known to simply race into the heart of the foe, smashing them apart before roaring off to the next target. Some lighter strike forces don't carry much heavy weaponry and so use Land Speeders, including the Ravenwing Vengeance variant, in an anti-tank role. In the skies above the battlefield, Nephilim Jetfighters are the bane of enemy flyers. Perhaps strangest of all is the floating reliquary known as the Darkshroud, its rippling force field offering protection to those nearby.

Working in conjunction, the Deathwing and Ravenwing strike like thunder and lightning, twin wings that envelop and destroy. First, the Ravenwing streak this way and that, an elusive foe that can dart in at any time like a rapier. Then,

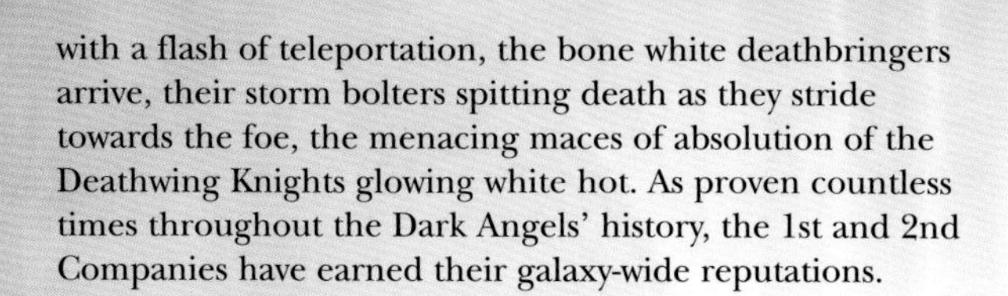

with a flash of teleportation, the bone white deathbringers arrive, their storm bolters spitting death as they stride towards the foe, the menacing maces of absolution of the Deathwing Knights glowing white hot. As proven countless times throughout the Dark Angels' history, the 1st and 2nd Companies have earned their galaxy-wide reputations.

The hunt for Elucidax the Keeper

Never has the reputation of the Deathwing and Ravenwing's joint operations been so well-illustrated as at the climax of the Altid Crusade. The Dark Angels committed to an assault upon the colony world of Altid 156, a planet populated by ragged pilgrim-colonists who had long since rejected the rule of Terra. Acting upon information that they never disclosed to the crusade's ruling council, the Dark Angels launched an assault by themselves.

The initial drop was carried out by Ravenwing squadrons who located the defensive bases of the colonists' command structure. The second phase of the assault was initiated according to the Chapter's highly effective doctrine. While the Ravenwing pinned down the enemy, elements of the 5th Company deployed via Thunderhawk gunship to establish a cordon around the enemy base and to engage outlying positions. Then, in response to the Ravenwing's homing signal, the Deathwing teleported directly into the foe's headquarters, laying down a fusillade of destruction and beginning their inexorable advance forwards to finish them.

At the battle's peak, the Deathwing met the foe they had really come to fight. The colonists were but chaff, although their leader, Elucidax the Keeper, was surrounded by a bodyguard of renegade Space Marines, traitors to the Emperor. Elucidax himself was an infamous heretic, known to have inspired dozens of rebellions across the quadrant. The Dark Angels knew Elucidax by another, older name: Zeriah, the one-time Master of the 14th Assault Company of the Dark Angels Legion.

Zeriah was a formidable opponent, and he killed a dozen Dark Angels and almost made good his escape before an assault cannon took him down, removing half of his chest in the process. An Apothecary rushed to ensure the traitor did not die. Too unstable to teleport, Zeriah was picked up by a Dark Talon and held within its stasis-crypt until they could make it back to the Rock. There, in one of the lowermost dungeons, the Interrogator-Chaplains were waiting.

A confession was extracted from the Fallen Dark Angel, although Zeriah refused to admit that joining Luther was wrong. For this, he was subjected to century-long torments; yet even to the bitter end, Zeriah remained unrepentant.

'Repent!... Repent!' The Master Interrogator-Chaplain's words echoed resoundingly off the rough walls of the cavernous cell. Rather than sounding like one man, the echoes created the impression that a whole army of Chaplains were interrogating the Space Marine. The Fallen Dark Angel said nothing.

The Chaplain paced across the stone floor before the restrained Dark Angel. The glow of halogen lamps reflected off the polished black surface of his armour while with one hand he toyed with the rosarius around his neck. Asmodai had served the Chapter for over a century, and in all that time only two of the Fallen had repented of their sins to him.

The Chaplain stopped in front of his prisoner and turned to face the broken warrior. Cold, dark eyes stared out from behind the skull-mask of Asmodai's armour. 'Repent!' he hissed.

The Fallen shut his eyes tight in an attempt to avoid the Interrogator's piercing gaze.

'Repent now and your death will be swift and relatively painless,' Asmodai stated coolly. 'Continue to refuse to admit your guilt and you will die in agony, the like of which you will only have imagined in your worst nightmares. The savagery of the Daemons of the Warp is nothing compared to the wrath of the Emperor!'

The Fallen Dark Angel opened his bloodshot eyes again and looked about him. The cold, unforgiving walls of the gloomy chamber held no encouragement. The imposing figure of the Master Interrogator-Chaplain glowered back at him.

The constant drip of water from the damp walls of the dungeon filled the captured Space Marine's ears. He closed his eyes, trying to shut out the sound of the water. The dripping became a tapping, the tapping a thumping until it was the panicked beating of his own heart pounding inside his head.

Shadows flickered and writhed across the fissured rock and the darkest shadow in the cell moved closer.

'Who is your lord?' demanded Asmodai.

'I have no lord and master.'

'The Emperor is your lord!'

'The Emperor rejected us, Chaos curse his soul,' whimpered the Fallen, his spirit on the verge of breaking. 'Lion El'Jonson betrayed us!'

'The Primarch is our saviour!' the Chaplain roared. 'The Lion sacrificed himself that the Order might survive. It is to him that we owe everything: our Chapter, our strength, our salvation, the very fibre of our being. And you dare say that you have no lord?' Asmodai spat, his growling whisper full of contempt.

The Fallen Dark Angel knew not how long he had been imprisoned within the Rock or for how many days the interrogation had lasted so far. All he knew now was that he just wanted to get away from the Chaplain's constant goading and torments. Restrained by the plasteel clamps, however, all he could do was turn his head away from his interrogator.

His voice composed again, Master Interrogator-Chaplain Asmodai spoke matter-of-factly in an emotionless tone as if he were reciting words he had uttered on countless occasions: 'As you will not admit to your wrong-doing and will not repent of your sins, it falls to me to relieve you of your guilt by whatever means are necessary.'

At that moment, the Fallen noticed the device the Chaplain had picked up in his other hand. Its many sharply-honed and polished blades gleamed red in the dim light.

'It is my sacred duty to save your soul from the Dark Gods of Chaos,' Asmodai intoned, 'and I will save your soul, even if you die in the process.'

HISTORY OF THE DARK ANGELS

Using the Rock as their mobile base, the Dark Angels have crisscrossed the galaxy bringing war to the Emperor's foes. Few Space Marine Chapters can match their roll call of victories – for they have fought in the forefront of many of the most crucial battles in the Imperium's history. For the Dark Angels, however, it is never enough – they remain the Unforgiven.

When the Dark Angels achieve a battlefield objective, they leave to seek their next engagement. They do not rebuild or perform humanitarian missions – they are the Emperor's warriors, made for war. They simply reclaim their stricken comrades and any prisoners they have taken before returning to their orbiting fleet.

As a rule, the secretive Dark Angels do not share battle records. They comply with the letter of the law for required reports, yet their communications are minimal. The Imperium's knowledge of the Chapter's plans and actions are vague, on par with only the Space Wolves, who are infamous for the utter disregard they show the bureaucrats of the Adeptus Administratum. The Imperium gleans much of its knowledge of the Dark Angels from outside reports, such as those submitted by Planetary Governors and Imperial Commanders who fought alongside them, or from the Inquisitors sent to inspect them.

With triumphs too numerous to list in full, the events detailed here are those battles that the Dark Angels themselves consider worthy of special commemoration.

120.M31 The Search for Recruiting Worlds
Necessity demands that the Dark Angels find a new recruiting world, but at this date, a conscious decision is made to establish many. This plan is agreed by the High Lords of Terra as it allows for contingencies and preserves genetic diversity. For the Dark Angels, it allows a mantle of secrecy, for no one is entirely sure of the number of recruiting worlds or of how many recruits are taken into the Rock.

580.M31-632.M32 The Forgotten Wars
Rumours lead the Dark Angels, with two of their Successor Chapters, to embark upon a harrowing campaign. In hindsight it is easy to see that the Ruinous Powers baited the Dark Angels, luring them into the swirling edge of the Eye of Terror. Only the Dark Angels' irrepressible resolve allows them to escape, and they pay a high price in casualties.

M31

M32

THE DAWNING OF THE IMPERIUM

There are few accurate records of this time, as the newborn Imperium of Mankind struggles to survive in the aftermath of the Horus Heresy.

There is no full account of the many battles fought during the Scouring.

c. M33 Missing Foundings
There are many Space Marine Foundings during this era, but the High Lords of Terra purposefully do not seek the gene-seed of the Dark Angels Chapter for any of them.

560.M33 2nd Mortis Gate Campaign
Almost the entire Dark Angels Chapter takes to the field, and it is recorded that all three of the Sacred Standards flew above the scene of that great triumph.

732.M33-822.M33 The Red Stars Campaign
In a series of wars, the mineral-rich Kulgotha system is scoured of xenos and claimed by the Imperium. The Dark Angels take part in many battles, including deploying in Chapter strength in the climactic battle of Vermilac Prime.

M33

THE FORGING

As the Imperium tightens the scrutiny under which citizen and soldier alike operate, the Dark Angels find themselves increasingly under observation. Only their flawless battle record and eagerness to combat the Imperium's enemies allows the Chapter to continue along its often secretive and mysterious path.

101.M34 Noble Passing
While leading his Chapter to victory in the Bloodpox Campaign against the Death Guard and the Brotherhood of Plague, the twelfth Supreme Grand Master of the Dark Angels, the esteemed Armaros contracts the loathsome pox. His rapid deformation convinces the Supreme Grand Master to immediately pass the Lion Helm to his successor. To ensure the contamination does not spread, Armaros voluntarily enters the Rock's reactor chamber and is wholly consumed.

456.M34 In the Wrong Hands
Inquisitor Halleck, after many decades tracking degenerates in wilderness space, captures a mysterious heretic known only as the Angel of Truth. The last broadcast by Halleck's ship claims the prisoner has broken under questioning and revealed deep-rooted heresy. While returning to Terra with his revelations, the Inquisitor is beset by an unknown enemy. The only Imperial force in the vicinity is the Dark Angels' strike cruiser, *Black Sword of Vengeance*. They report no sign of the Inquisitor, his vessel or the prisoner.

104.M35 The Enemy Unmasked
The Dark Angels, following Cypher's trail, are led to believe that at least one member of the newly declared Ur-Council of Nova Terra is a Fallen Dark Angel. In a daring raid, a Ravenwing strike force lands upon Nova Terra but fails to secure any prisoners.

495.M35 The Deathwing Unleashed
Segmentum Pacificus is the centre of unrest and the Inner Circle continues to follow the many clues that have led them deep into the internecine fighting. Known to the Dark Angels as the Hrakon Campaign, they systematically seek out Obidiah Hrakon, the despot ruler of an upstart planet, which has been pivotal in its support of Nova Terra. In the Veiled Region, the Dark Angels finally corner Hrakon, who takes refuge on a piratical port world. Seeking to ensure that none escape, the Dark Angels blockade the planet and unleash the entire Deathwing. Deploying in sequential teleportations, the Terminators prosecute an epic slaughter until only a single foe is left alive – Obidiah Hrakon – once a standard bearer for the Dark Angels Legion. Refusing to give up, Obidiah is subdued after a duel with the Master of the Deathwing and is transported back to the Rock. His death is not an easy one.

975.M35 Brother Against Brother
Still operating largely in Segmentum Pacificus, the Dark Angels take part in the fierce fighting of the Cataclysm of Souls. In addition to putting down those who reject the High Lords of Terra and the Ecclesiarchy, they search for signs of the Fallen. It is a civil war the like of which the Imperium has not seen since the Horus Heresy.

980.M35 Hrud Rising
The Dark Angels take part in the task force cleansing the Hrud infestations that erupt across the Imperium. With two of their three assigned sectors cleared, the Rock disappears as the Dark Angels leave the campaign to pursue their own objectives. The Chapter Master of the Ultramarines files a complaint to the High Lords of Terra, although no action is seen to be taken.

314.M36-334.M36 The Trail of Unbelief
The Dark Angels begin a two decade long campaign beset with many battles to hunt down Brother Machius, a former lieutenant of Cardinal Bucharis. Despite several ambushes set by the Night Lords Traitor Legion, the Dark Angels prevail – the Ravenwing locate Machius on the plague-ridden planet of Gronmoth, capturing him at the Battle of Black Death.

439.M36 The Rebulus Cleansing
Following a mysterious trail, the Dark Angels and several of their Successor Chapters begin a 30-year campaign that uproots hidden cults and corrupt officials across three sectors. The battles against this network of subversion bring much suffering to the Rebulus system before the corruption is finally subdued, culminating in the destruction of the artificial moons surrounding the planet Ixx.

673.M36 Siege of Dominus Prime
The Dark Angels and Angels of Vengeance both deploy their entire 1st Companies to end the five year deadlock against a rebel tyrant. Nigh on two hundred Terminators crack open the 'unassailable' fortress and massacre the traitors, save for those few who are taken to the Rock for questioning.

M34

M35

M36

THE TIME OF SCHISMS

This is an era riven by civil war, as the Imperium withstands both the Nova Terra Interregnum and the dissent known as the Age of Apostasy. Many of the Fallen surface during this time, often as the leaders inciting the many rebellions. The Dark Angels and their Successor Chapters cross the galaxy in countless actions, ruthlessly hunting down cult leaders.

551.M37 Kurin's Acropolis
The battle honours of the 3rd Company are many, but few evoke more hard-won pride than the lone ribbon that commemorates the battle for Kurin's Acropolis on Persembe II. After making a daring Drop Pod assault to create a cordon between the acropolis and the encroaching horde of Daemons and cultists, the Dark Angels slay the vile sorcerer, High Anarchist Potchek, to end the threat.

871.M37 The Battle of Midpoint
An Eldar fleet threatens to destroy the massive space docks of Midpoint in the Argonnes sector. The sudden appearance of the Rock and the Dark Angels' Swordfleet tips the battle in the Imperium's favour. The Eldar retreat, but not before the firepower of the Rock annihilates their capital ship and a half dozen vessels of their armada. To this day, the savaged hulls and floating corpses of both sides hang in the depths of space, forming an eternal graveyard.

883.M37 Betrayal at Zambeque
The Ravenwing follow a trail that leads all the way to the Imperial Governor of Zambeque, a key Imperial planet sometimes called the gateway to the Gothic sector. Before they can apprehend the Governor for questioning, however, the planet declares open rebellion. The Dark Angels task force is surrounded upon Zambeque by traitor marines of the Alpha Legion, and only the timely counter strike by half of the Deathwing prevents the annihilation of the 5th Company. The Governor, a Fallen Angel who was once Brother Solas, escapes with the remnants of his Chaos Space Marines allies.

987.M37 Grim Reaping
After picking up the trail of Brother Solas, the entire Ravenwing deploys en masse on the plains of Picus, an agri world in the Orar sub-sector. All ten Dark Shrouds join the hunt, bringing a shroud of unnatural darkness to the planet's sun-drenched surface that can be seen from orbit. Despite their sweeping efforts, Brother Solas evades them again, and the Chapter records state that Cypher himself may have had a hand in Solas' uncanny escape.

299.M38-309.M38 Altid Crusade
The Dark Angels were a crucial part of the Altid Crusade, a decade long campaign that ended on the colony world of Altid 156. Although their rapid actions to complete the mission were not coordinated with the rest of the forces of the Imperium, the Dark Angels' success in slaying the heretic leader Elucidax the Keeper ensured that despite the breach in protocol, no inquiries would be made.

666.M38 The Blackest Time
Three Grand Masters of the Ravenwing are lost in a single year, each slain while in pursuit of a group of Fallen Dark Angels. This marks the beginning of an unprecedented two-decade period where the Ravenwing has no Grand Master. During this time, the Ravenwing are given direct orders from the Master of the 2nd Company of the Angels of Vengeance, as the Dark Angels wait until a suitable candidate can be found from within their own ranks.

519.M39 The Hundred Planet Rebellion
While attempting to follow Cypher's path, the Dark Angels uncover a mad priest named Alldric the Subverter. The heretic visionary has led a swathe of planets on the borders of the Veiled Region to reject the rule of the Imperium. Within a decade, the Dark Angels, and several of their Successor Chapters, suppress the cultist uprisings and slay their leaders.

891.M39 The Lost Hope of Perdition
A Dark Angels' investigation of a space hulk newly materialised out of the Warp discovers strong elements of the renegades known as the Cleaved. The ensuing fight is won when Assault Squads, advancing behind a trio of Dreadnoughts, get close enough to set cyclonic charges in the engine rooms.

550.M40 Destruction of Grymm's Landing
One of the first and most reliable of the Dark Angels' recruiting worlds is destroyed in an uprising, instigated by the Alpha Legion and supported by the Night Lords.

M37 M38 M39 M40

AGE OF REDEMPTION

As the Imperium attempts to mortify the many sins committed during the previous Age of Apostasy, the Dark Angels enter into a period of their history which they know as the Time of a Thousand Crusades. Broken into more numerous, but smaller, strike forces, the Chapter disperses across the galaxy in order to confront a greater number of threats. It is, however, a largely fallow period where the Hunt for the Fallen is concerned, and the Chapter endures more fruitless rumours and dead ends than successful investigations.

405.M41 Macharian Heresy
Over three decades, the Dark Angels are tasked with suppressing the civil wars that are ongoing across many of the territories gained during the Macharian Conquests. The Ravenwing uncover several corrupt cults, largely instigated by the Alpha Legion, and the unmistakable signs of Cypher's presence. During the Lythanos Uprisings, only a run-in with the Space Wolves allows several Fallen to escape.

780.M41 The Fourth Quadrant Rebellion
Over ten years, a series of wars engulf a quarter of Segmentum Solar. The Dark Angels take part in several battles, supressing the Egammonon Revolt, halting the invasion of Rastabal, and assaulting the fortress of Kaligar.

832.M41 Massacre on Minoria
The 1st Company deploys en masse to kill or capture every inhabitant of the moon of Minoria in the Periliac System. It is claimed by several other Space Marine Chapters that the Dark Angels' presence was needed on Periliac Prime which was, at the time, beset by Waaagh! Drillakilla.

897.M41 Faze Uprising
A Dark Angels strike force explores a region previously covered by Warp storms. On the surface of Faze V, they are engaged by cybernetically-altered men in the thrall of a blasphemous machine intelligence. The Dark Angels attack the logic-engines and free the population from the AI's control, but they crave their machine-ruler and reject freedom. The Dark Angels press their attack. In a gruelling campaign, the techno-recidivists of Faze V are eventually wiped off the face of their world.

922.M41 The Toxic World of Sephlagm
The 3rd and 4th Companies pin down a cultist army while the Ravenwing deploys in a pincer formation. Support Squadrons clear streets while Attack Squadrons rush the rebel headquarters, summoning the Deathwing to take out the possessed rebel leader.

939.M41 Death of the Supreme Grand Master
Whilst pursuing Cypher, Commander Naberius – Supreme Grand Master of the Dark Angels – is led into an ambush and slain by Chaos Space Marines. Azrael leads the Deathwing to recover his body, and is subsequently named as his successor.

949.M41 Waaagh! Groblinik
Fighting alongside the Vostroyan Firstborn, Mordian Iron Guard and the Adeptus Mechanicus Skitarii legions, the Dark Angels attempt to halt the onslaught of Waaagh! Groblinik. The Orks are checked at the Battle of the Sularian Gate and Ezekiel, Grand Master of Librarians, slays Warlord Groblinik.

989.M41 Rynn's World and Bad Landing
A Dark Angels strike force, including the entire Ravenwing, is sent to aid the Crimson Fists and reconquer the worlds in the Loki Sector under Ork domination.

996.M41 Cleansing of Durganion XIII
A distress call lures a Dark Angels strike force into a Genestealer ambush, and the confines of the hive prove an advantage to the xenos. The battle ends when the Broodlord is destroyed by a Ravenwing advance. Without his guidance, the remaining xenos are exterminated and the planet marked for corruption testing.

221997.M41 Storm of Vengeance
The Waaagh! of Ghazghkull Thraka and Nazdreg invades Piscina IV.

997.M41 Third Tyrannic War
Several Dark Angels strike forces take part in fighting the far-reaching tendrils of Hive Fleet Leviathan.

998.M41 To Catch Cypher
The Black Templars fight alongside the Dark Angels, though a dispute over a Black Templars prisoner causes both Chapters to briefly engage. The incident is reported to Terra and Inquisitor Archibald is assigned to lead the inquiry.

884999.M41 Dark Vengeance
The Dark Angels 5th Company battles elements of the Crimson Slaughter for control of the Hellfire Stone.

995999.M41 The 13th Black Crusade
Abaddon's dreaded 13th Black Crusade pours out of the Eye of Terror. According to the Dark Oracle, many Fallen are among them, so the Rock makes all speed for the Cadian sector.

THE DAYS OF JUDGEMENT

During the latter days of the 41st Millennium, the Dark Angels have become embroiled in an unrelenting period of war after war. Distress calls and pleas for help bombard the Rock's Astropaths as countless enemies beset the whole of the Imperium of Mankind. Each segmentum reports rebellions, xenos attacks and growing Warp rifts in unprecedented numbers. With humanity itself besieged, the Unforgiven Chapters, or at least rumours of them, seem to be everywhere during this period.

The End is Nigh

Many say this is the Time of Ending and that Mankind stands upon the twilight of its last battle. Across the galaxy, prophets and augurs predict impending doom for humanity, foretelling the coming dominance of xenos races or, it is whispered, something much worse...

Even as the Rock makes haste towards the embattled Cadian sector, the Chapter is bombarded with distress calls; urgent pleas for aid from desperate planets. The Inner Circle is awash with confirmed reports of the Fallen, including Cypher himself. The psychic choir has become so overloaded with messages of xenos invasions and uprisings that it is impossible to track which are current and which are ghost messages – lingering echoes of bygone disasters. On countless planets of the Imperium, despair hangs overhead as thick as the recycled atmosphere of an overcrowded hive world. From the psi-shielded sanctum of the Librarius, Ezekiel, the Grand Master of Librarians, reports a tide of Warp energies rising, the Eye of Terror once more spewing forth its filth into the galaxy, including the unmistakable signs of the Fallen amongst their number.

Desperate to capture the Fallen and to prevent any from revealing the Chapter's long-kept secret, the Dark Angels are already too thinly spread. Risking the scrutiny of the Inquisition and the allegation of legion-building, the Dark Angels call upon their Successor Chapters for aid. The Unforgiven gird for battle as never before. Into this scene of growing calamity, Supreme Grand Master Azrael emerges from the deepest dungeon of the Rock, his keen mind still attempting to decipher the gibbering deluge of information spouted by the Dark Oracle. Despite the multitude of threats and darkness of the hour, this is what the Space Marines were made for, and they do not shirk before war's calling.

Brooding and perhaps obsessively flawed by past failings, the Dark Angels nevertheless rush once more to the forefront of Mankind's battle for survival. There, they will fight with righteous fervour and a stubborn refusal to accept defeat, whatever the odds, whoever the enemy.

MASTER OF THE ROCK

Most Space Marine Chapters have a Master of the Forge; the most senior Techmarine. With deep understanding of the arcane sciences refined over many years of experience, the Master of the Forge is comparable to a Tech-Priest of the Adeptus Mechanicus. The Dark Angels have a similar role, known as the Master of the Rock, although there is an ominous difference. Upon ascending to the honoured position, the Master of the Rock follows his predecessors by being permanently wired into the control nave of machine banks located deep within the asteroid base. It is his solemn duty to placate the most important machine spirits, directing the maintenance of the engines and Warp drive that allow the enormous asteroid to travel the galaxy. It is his mind alone that perceives the workings of the force field that still shields the asteroid base. The previous Masters, whose fleshly bodies have withered, are left in place, their mechanical upgrades still working while bones fall in dusty heaps below. Eventually, they will be collected for display in the Alcoves of Honour. Because of their dual allegiance to the Chapter and the Adeptus Mechanicus, Techmarines are never inducted into the Deathwing. This includes the Master of the Rock; he is privy only to the secrets of their asteroid base and its hoard of ancient technology.

The Final Secret

For nearly 10,000 years, the Dark Angels have kept the secret of the disastrous events that took place on Caliban. They will never reveal the truth to anyone outside their Chapter, for they could not bear for others to know their terrible shame. And all the while, deep within the Rock, his continued existence known only to the Watchers in the Dark and the Supreme Grand Master, the arch-traitor Luther raves on – speaking of what is to come or emitting senseless shrieks. At times, his voice assumes a grating, inhuman quality and it tells cunning lies or speaks words of such utter despair that to hear them is to wish for death. It is the rare moments of lucidity, when Luther begs for his own end, that are, perhaps, the hardest to endure – although each and every Supreme Grand Master has done so. They hope to gain wisdom from this darksome oracle, hoping to hear Luther recant, so that he might be, at last, released. Yet even the highest-ranking Dark Angels do not know everything, although they think that they do...

Buried yet deeper within the Rock, hidden in its innermost chamber, is the final, greatest secret of the Dark Angels.

Only one person in the galaxy knows the full truth – the Emperor. Even in his living entombment upon the Golden Throne, even though the sunken orbits of his skull no longer have eyes, the Emperor still sees much. Hidden inside a secluded chamber at the heart of what was once the planet of Caliban, unreachable by all save the cryptic Watchers in the Dark, the mighty Primarch Lion El'Jonson lies sleeping. There he slumbers, his wounds long-healed, waiting for that time when he will be needed once again, when the clarion call of battle sounds for the last time, summoning him to once again defend the Imperium of Mankind against its enemies.

The Unforgiven

This section of the book details the forces used by the Dark Angels – their weapons, their units and the special characters that lead them to war. Each entry describes a unit and gives the specific rules you will need to use it in your games. The army list (pages 90-104) refers back to these entries.

DARK ANGELS SPECIAL RULES

The Dark Angels army uses a number of special rules that are common to several of its units. These are collected and explained here, in full, for your convenience. Special rules that are unique to particular units are presented in the relevant entry instead. Other, more common, rules are simply listed by name – these are described in full in the Special Rules section of your *Warhammer 40,000* rulebook.

Combat Squads

It is sound doctrine for units to remain flexible, splitting into two entities as the tactical situation dictates.

A ten-man unit with this special rule can break down into two five-man units, called combat squads.

You must decide which units are splitting into combat squads, and which models go into each combat squad, immediately before deployment. A unit split into combat squads, therefore, is now two separate units for all game purposes, including calculating the total number of units in the army and the number of units you can place in reserve. Then proceed with deployment as normal. Note that two combat squads split from the same unit can embark in the same Transport vehicle, providing its Transport Capacity allows.

Once you have decided whether or not to split a unit into combat squads, it must remain that way for the entire battle. It cannot split up or join back together later on in the game, nor can you use a redeployment to split up a unit or join it back together.

Grim Resolve

The Dark Angels are renowned for being tenacious and taciturn, making them hard to repulse in battle. However, such an intractable nature also means they will keep on fighting even when discretion might prove the better part of valour.

A model with the Grim Resolve special rule has the Stubborn special rule.

In addition, a unit containing at least one model with the Grim Resolve special rule can never choose to automatically fail a Morale check.

Inner Circle

Dark Angels veterans of unquestionable battle prowess and devotion are promoted into the 1st Company. Further training steels their minds to continue the long war for the Chapter's redemption.

A model with this special rule has the Fearless and Preferred Enemy (Chaos Space Marines) special rules.

Warlord Traits Table

When generating his Warlord Traits, a Dark Angels Warlord may either roll on one of the Warlord Traits tables in the *Warhammer 40,000* rulebook, or instead roll on the table below.

D6	WARLORD TRAIT
1	**Rapid Manoeuvre:** *This Warlord is known for his ability to rapidly deploy into ideal attack positions.* Your Warlord, and any unit he joins, can either roll 2 dice when they Run, using the highest roll, or can add D6" to any Turbo-boost they make (or Flat Out move, in the case of Master Sammael on his Land Speeder).
2	**The Hunt:** *The path of one of the Fallen, perhaps even Cypher himself, has crossed this battlefield – more information must be extracted from the enemy leaders.* If your Warlord, or the unit he is with, slays the enemy Warlord in the Assault phase, you score an additional Victory Point.
3	**Courage of the Lion:** *Since the Great Crusade, the Dark Angels have been famous for standing fast beside their leaders.* The Warlord, and all friendly units within 12" of him, roll an additional dice when making Leadership tests, discarding the highest.
4	**For the Lion!** *It is a leader's duty to inspire his battle-brothers to greatness through the courage and daring of his own actions.* The Warlord and his unit have the Furious Charge special rule.
5	**Brilliant Planning:** *The Sons of the Lion have inherited some of their Primarch's vaunted ability to coordinate attacks.* While the Warlord is alive, you can increase or decrease each of your Reserves rolls by 1 (choose after you roll the dice).
6	**Hold At All Costs:** *Upon securing objectives pivotal to the Chapter's aims, a commander can call upon the Dark Angels' notoriously tenacious defence, fending off superior numbers through sheer force of will.* The Warlord, and any Dark Angels unit he is in, has the Feel No Pain special rule whilst they are within 3" of an objective.

Company Masters

LORDS OF THE UNFORGIVEN, KEEPERS OF A SECRET KEY

To lead the Dark Angels requires a battle-hardened veteran, a dedicated warrior who has proven his prowess and Chapter loyalty a thousand times over. Such heroes advance into the fabled Deathwing, the 1st Company, but in order to be considered for command, a Space Marine must distinguish himself yet further. Only those who show superlative leadership and tactical skills, who prove themselves to be the best of the best, can ever rise to become a Company Master.

The Dark Angels do not call their leaders by the typical designation of Captain, preferring instead to retain their old Order titles of Company Master. Each of the ten companies of the Dark Angels is led by such a Master, who ultimately fall under the command of the Supreme Grand Master. Each Company Master bears additional honorific titles, reflective of his solemn duties within the Chapter.

All Dark Angels are taciturn and monastic in nature, and these traits are exemplified by their Company Masters. They shun highly visible, diplomatic roles, avoiding even well-deserved battle laurels and adulation. Where the lauded Captains of other Space Marine Chapters deliver rousing speeches to coalition forces of the Imperium, the leaders of the Dark Angels are shadowy figures, more comfortable in cowled reclusion than at the forefront, acting as a skilled orator. Yet for all their silent reservations, Company Masters are no less commanding, though perhaps their grim silence makes them somehow more menacing.

With a signal, a Company Master launches the Emperor's finest into action. None can claim to be more disciplined than the Dark Angels; a single barked order can start any number of flawlessly executed manoeuvres. Almost soundlessly, attack plans are orchestrated and fire support coordinated. A Company Master meets each challenge with the same intractable resolve. Such leaders are not only superb strategists, but also the most skilled of combatants. Armed with the finest wargear from the Rock's armoury, and with relics maintained since the dawn of the Imperium, a Company Master can cleave through alien hordes or cut down even the mightiest foe in a personal challenge.

As part of the Inner Circle, a Company Master may join his 1st Company brethren in battle, donning his Terminator armour and leading one of the most feared fighting formations in the galaxy. However, they are most assured in the midst of their own troops, leading their Company to victory in the name of the Emperor and the Lion of Caliban.

The Company Masters know they and their battle-brothers are descended from the First Legion, the first of the Emperor's Space Marines, the Sons of the Lion. They know theirs is a heavy responsibility, for it is their role to both uphold the awe-inspiring honour of the Dark Angels, while at the same time seeking to exorcise the secret sins of the past. On their orders will the Chapter attain victories, and through them, final redemption.

	WS	BS	S	T	W	I	A	Ld	Sv
Company Master	6	5	4	4	3	5	3	10	3+

UNIT TYPE: **Infantry (Character).**

WARGEAR: **Power armour** (pg 65)**, bolt pistol, chainsword, frag grenades, krak grenades, iron halo** (pg 63).

SPECIAL RULES: **Independent Character, Inner Circle** (pg 28).

WATCHERS IN THE DARK

The diminutive, hooded attendants that cluster around the highest-ranking warriors of the Dark Angels have long been a mystery to onlookers. These are the Watchers in the Dark, but none can say for certain what manner of creature lies beneath those robes. Whatever they are, they speak no words. Their presence is solemnly accepted, if never visibly acknowledged – like some omnipresent manifestation of guilt, a burden clothed in monastic robes that glides closest to those privy to the Chapter's most terrible secrets.

Chaplains & Interrogator-Chaplains

KEEPERS OF CHAPTER PURITY, SHEPHERDS OF THE INCORRUPTIBLE

The Space Marine Legions were created long before the development of the Imperial Creed and the dominion of the Adeptus Ministorum. As a result, every Space Marine Chapter had its own cult practices and its own attendant priests. These spiritual leaders of the Space Marines are known as Chaplains, and for over ten thousand years, they have led the holy rites of their Chapters.

Dark Angels' Chaplains are the keepers of the Reclusiam, the central shrine within the Rock. They emerge to preside over ancient ceremonies – inducting neophytes into the Chapter with Rites of Initiation, steeling the hearts and minds of recruits and veterans alike with the Vows of Intolerance, and leading all through prayers of dedication to battle, Primarch and Emperor. A Chaplain instils strict discipline in his brothers, armouring them within through tenet and catechism. The monastic Dark Angels are inundated with rituals, and it is the Chaplain's role to screen his brethren, watching for even the smallest failing in humility or mental fortitude.

Chaplains are daunting figures, for their jet black livery is adorned with icons of battle and mysterious tokens of ritual. Their skull helms at once evoke the stern image of the immortal Emperor and the grim promise of death. In the midst of battle, a Chaplain is truly in his element, preaching the righteous work of warfare, chanting Liturgies of Battle and punctuating his sermons with deadly strikes from his blazing crozius arcanum – the skull-headed cudgel that is both a Chaplain's badge of office and chosen weapon.

If a Dark Angels Chaplain can prove himself through years of heroic service, he might be found worthy of acceptance into the Inner Circle. After an arcane and convoluted ceremony in the Hall of Secrets, deep in the bowels of the Rock, the Chaplain is given the Test of Faith. Failures are led further into the dungeons and never seen again, but should he pass, he takes the solemn vow of the Deathwing and will henceforth be given the title of Interrogator-Chaplain. In addition to their previous role, it is the sacred duty of Interrogator-Chaplains to make any of the Fallen who are captured repent. This requires a will of unbreakable adamant, as the horrific acts of forcing repentance are not an easy burden to bear. Interrogator-Chaplains must weather heretical ranting and lies, discern insincere bleating and remain steadfast in their commitment to compel contrition from the lips of traitors. The Fallen who repent are rewarded with a quick death, whilst those who do not are shown ever more drastic measures that eventually lead to the same destination, but take considerably longer in the journey.

	WS	BS	S	T	W	I	A	Ld	Sv
Chaplain	5	4	4	4	2	4	2	10	3+
Interrogator-Chaplain	5	5	4	4	3	5	3	10	3+

UNIT TYPE: **Infantry (Character).**

WARGEAR: **Power armour** (pg 65), **bolt pistol, crozius arcanum** (pg 62), **frag grenades, krak grenades, rosarius** (pg 64).

SPECIAL RULES: **Independent Character, Inner Circle** (Interrogator-Chaplain only) (pg 28), **Zealot.**

THE BLACK PEARLS

An Interrogator-Chaplain can add a single black pearl to his rosarius for each of the Fallen that he convinces to repent. Master Molochia, inarguably the greatest of his grim profession, died after over 300 years of service with only ten black pearls. To this day, no other has been able to emulate his achievement. The black pearls themselves can only be found on the planet of Malmar, a watery death world on the edge of the Eye of Terror. Upon promotion to his role, each Interrogator-Chaplain must travel to Malmar to retrieve one of these treasures to be stored within the Reclusiam, in the hope that one day it will be returned. It is said that on that dread planet, one must face his own temptations – a test of will that makes the threat of the fierce predators seem easy by comparison.

Librarians

Many recruits do not survive the process that transforms them into Space Marines, and fewer still can endure what it takes to become a Space Marine Librarian. To prevent the spread of mutation, each Chapter subjects their initiates to testing so rigorous that it is in itself life-threatening. Such precautions are warranted, for the consequences of corrupted gene-seed would be dire. Most neophytes who are suspected of being a psyker by the repeated screenings are given their last rites and slain outright. Some few are spared, and allowed to continue their Space Marine inductions, albeit under even harsher scrutiny.

The majority of those with psychic ability do not have the cerebral fortitude or immense willpower to control their mental forces. To assess their resolve, those especially marked initiates are subjected to additional batteries of new tests: mind-moulding sessions that attempt to break their sanity, temptations that lure the wavering, and mental barrages that overwhelm the unfocused. Most recruits are ruined in these stages, their weak wills betraying their flaws and dooming them to another fate entirely – there is only one solution for psykers who cannot be fully trusted. Yet some of the recruits are strengthened by their mental ordeals, and are thus allowed to continue.

The extra testing and more rigorous sanctions are put in place because psykers are naturally unstable, and their untutored powers leave them as conduits to apocalyptic dangers. The mind of a psyker registers strongly in the Warp, and should that spark attract the unwanted attention of the fiendish denizens of that murky realm, it is possible for the psyker to be driven insane or become possessed. In such cases, psykers can be manipulated into doing great evils or, in the worst instance, tearing open the veil between realspace and the Warp in a full scale daemonic incursion, threatening planets and entire star systems.

Those who prove strong enough to accept the transplants and upgrades to their physical and mental abilities find themselves in training to be Librarians, mystic Space Marine warriors who can wield awesome mental powers. In battle, Librarians can send out blasting psychic bolts to strike down their foes, halt war engines with but a gesture, or project near-impenetrable force domes to protect their allies. Besides lending their might in war, Librarians have other duties to the Chapter. They are the official record keepers of the Chapter, and it is not unusual to find them liaising with officers and leaders, for they have unnatural intuitive powers – sometimes able to pluck thoughts from the minds of their foes or use auguring skills to detect an enemy's movements. Librarians are also pivotal in the role of interstellar communications, able to project their thoughts across time and space, sending and receiving messages to far-distant Astropath stations or other members of the Chapter. Dark Angels Librarians are also called upon when questioning the Fallen, working alongside the Ravenwing and Interrogator-Chaplains, using their powers to weaken prisoners' mental defences and sift out deception.

Although accepted by their brethren, something keeps Librarians apart from their fellow Space Marines, isolated even within a squad. Perhaps it is because psykers are generally abhorred within the Imperium, or maybe it is out of awe for a figure who can stop incoming shells with his mind and seems privy to one's innermost thoughts.

	WS	BS	S	T	W	I	A	Ld	Sv
Librarian	5	4	4	4	2	4	2	10	3+

UNIT TYPE: **Infantry (Character).**

WARGEAR: **Power armour** (pg 65), **bolt pistol, force weapon, frag grenades, krak grenades, psychic hood.**

SPECIAL RULES: **Independent Character, Inner Circle** (pg 28), **Psyker (Mastery Level 1).**

PSYKER: Dark Angels Librarians generate their powers from the **Divination**, **Pyromancy**, **Telepathy**, and **Telekinesis** disciplines.

Techmarines

Keeping wargear and fighting vehicles at peak efficiency while being on campaign for months or even years at a time is no easy task, for the wear of battle grinds down even the toughest constructs. It is a Techmarine's sacred duty to ensure his brethren's ability to wage war is never diminished.

Ancient pacts allow Space Marines to send warriors with technological aptitude to study the ways of the Machine God. Aspiring Dark Angels Techmarines train for thirty years on Mars, learning rites of activation, hymnals of maintenance and the correct methods of calling forth a machine spirit or placating its wrath. After instruction, they return to the Rock, though they are never again fully accepted by their brethren, for Dark Angels are ever dubious of outside influences. The Techmarines suffer this stigma with dignity and pride, for they know that their role is essential to the battle-readiness of the Chapter.

When assigned to a strike force, a Techmarine accompanies his brothers into action, for he is a warrior first and foremost. There, he ministers to sundered vehicles and retrieves prized wargear with a ferocity hitherto unseen by his comrades.

	WS	BS	S	T	W	I	A	Ld	Sv
Techmarine	4	4	4	4	1	4	1	8	2+

UNIT TYPE: **Infantry (Character).**

WARGEAR: **Artificer armour** (pg 65), **bolt pistol, servo-arm** (pg 62), **frag grenades, krak grenades.**

SPECIAL RULES: **And They Shall Know No Fear, Grim Resolve** (pg 28), **Independent Character.**

Blessing of the Omnissiah: In each of your Shooting phases, instead of firing his weapons, a Techmarine may choose to repair a single friendly vehicle that he is in base contact with or embarked upon. To repair a vehicle, roll a D6 and add the following modifiers where applicable:

- Each servitor with a servo-arm in his unit +1
- The Techmarine has a servo-harness +1

If the result is 5 or more, you may either restore a Hull Point lost earlier in the battle, or repair a Weapon Destroyed or Immobilised result suffered earlier in the battle; this is effective immediately.

Bolster Defences: After deployment, but before Scout redeployments and Infiltrate deployments, nominate one piece of terrain in your deployment zone (this may not be one you have purchased as part of your army). The terrain piece's cover save is increased by one for the duration of the game (to a maximum of 3+). For example, a ruin (4+ cover save) would instead offer a 3+ cover save. A piece of terrain can only be bolstered once.

SERVITORS

To undertake manual labour, the Techmarines create cyborg Servitors from neophytes who fail in their training. Physically strong, with limited cognitive abilities, they serve the Chapter – if in a much less glorious way than their brethren.

	WS	BS	S	T	W	I	A	Ld	Sv
Servitor	3	3	3	3	1	3	1	8	4+

UNIT TYPE: **Infantry.**

WARGEAR: **Servo-arm** (pg 62).

SPECIAL RULES:
Mindlock: Unless it includes a Techmarine, an unengaged unit that contains at least one model with this special rule must roll a D6 at the start of its turn. On a roll of a 4+, there is no effect this turn. On a roll of a 1, 2 or 3, the unit is mindlocked until the start of its following turn. A mindlocked unit may not voluntarily move, shoot or charge. A mindlocked unit must still complete compulsory moves, such as Pile In and Fall Back moves.

Command Squads

The highest-ranking Dark Angels are often accompanied by a Command Squad – a hand-picked unit of the five most able Company Veterans. The Codex Astartes sanctions the formation of these units largely as bodyguards for key Masters of the Chapter.

Dark Angels leaders use their Command Squads in a variety of roles, such as forming honour guards to spearhead attacks, shoring up defensive lines, or achieving special missions. Because of their elite nature, Command Squads can draw upon the Rock's full arsenal of weaponry and equipment. The most prominent addition to any Command Squad is the standard bearer, for he carries one of the company's much-revered banners. Since the Rock was made the Dark Angels' base of operations, the solemn Great Hall has been lined with proud company standards, along with ceremonial banners, heraldic pennants and, in pride of place, the Sacred Standards. Every Son of the Lion, from neophyte to the most battle-scarred veteran, will fight even harder beneath the august presence of such a Chapter icon. Whether it is a Company Master leading a Command Squad with its Company Standard into the thick of the fighting, or the bearer of a Sacred Standard marking the Dark Angels' hold over a rallying point, the heraldry of the Dark Angels is a call to war that is known and feared across the galaxy.

Some Command Squads contain a specialist known as an Apothecary – a battle-brother versed in the arts of combat medical aid. Working in the front lines, an Apothecary will use his narthecium – a field kit that contains all the tech, stim-packs and sacred unguents needed to patch wounds – allowing his brethren to return to battle. Not all the wounded can be saved, but between their ceramite armour, hale constitutions and self-healing bio-properties, only the most horrific of wounds are mortal. When an Apothecary finds one past hope, he will calm the dying, perhaps helping them on their way with a deft cut, and take out his reductor. This special device from his narthecium is used to remove progenoid organs. From the secrets held within these organs, future generations of Space Marines are created, and the continuation of the Chapter is assured.

A Command Squad can also contain a Company Champion. In the Dark Angels Chapter, each company has unique rituals – most often some combination of duels, contests of strength, and mind battles of self-control. The winners of such competitions represent their company during the ceremonies held in the Great Hall of the Rock. These individuals embody the honour of their company, representing their brothers in the mysteries of rites as they do in war. On the battlefield, it is a Company Champion's task to personally confront enemy warlords and captains, leaving the Company Master free to conduct the wider battle. Should the Dark Angels encounter Space Wolves during their missions, it is a Company Champion who will face the Space Wolves' champion in ritual combat, re-enacting the epic clash fought between their respective Primarchs nearly 10,000 years ago.

	WS	BS	S	T	W	I	A	Ld	Sv
Veteran	4	4	4	4	1	4	2	9	3+
Company Champion	5	4	4	4	1	4	2	9	3+
Apothecary	4	4	4	4	1	4	2	9	3+

UNIT TYPE: **Infantry.** Company Champion and Apothecary are **Infantry (Character).**

WARGEAR:

Veteran: **Power armour** (pg 65)**, bolt pistol, chainsword, frag grenades, krak grenades.**

Company Champion: **Power armour** (pg 65)**, bolt pistol, blade of Caliban** (pg 62)**, frag grenades, krak grenades, combat shield** (pg 63)**.**

Apothecary: **Power armour** (pg 65)**, chainsword, frag grenades, krak grenades, narthecium** (pg 63)**.**

SPECIAL RULES: **And They Shall Know No Fear, Grim Resolve** (pg 28)**.**

Dark Angels Space Marines

Each Dark Angels Space Marine is a genetically engineered giant that has undergone the most rigorous training and is girded for war with the finest equipment in Mankind's domain. He is the equal of dozens, if not a hundred lesser soldiers. As set down in the Codex Astartes, Dark Angels are organised into three main types of squad: Tactical, Assault and Devastator. Each is led by a Sergeant and includes nine other Space Marines, although they may split into sub-units called combat squads, to allow greater battlefield flexibility.

TACTICAL SQUADS

Tactical Squads are the backbone of the Dark Angels army. They are versatile warriors, able and equipped to perform a number of battlefield roles. A Tactical Squad could be asked to hold ground, provide fire support, charge into melee, or perhaps do all during the course of the same battle. Adaptability is the hallmark of Tactical Squads. Other Space Marine squads are optimised to perform a single task, but the flexible Tactical Squad is built around the premise that its role will change based on need – fluidly switching from offense to defence, from static to mobile, from ranged combat to close assault. The circumstances of a battle will dictate the course of action they should follow.

The armament carried by a Tactical Squad is the boltgun, the standard anti-personnel weapon of choice and bringer of death to the Emperor's enemies since the Great Crusade. As befits its needs, a Tactical Squad will supplement its firepower with more specialised or heavier weaponry – such as a flamer to cleanse foes from cover, or a plasma cannon, to combat heavily armoured enemies. Every battle-brother is fully trained with the entire arsenal, as such duties are rotated to ensure the various firearm skills remain sharp. Tactical Squads often take to battle within a Rhino or perhaps a Razorback, as these tracked transports better allow for rapid redeployment or the seizure of vital objectives.

No matter the foe, no matter the odds, the Dark Angels fight with tenacity. This grim determination was perhaps best exemplified by the Tactical Squads of the 3rd Company when they faced the onslaught of Ghazghkull Thraka's Orks in the confines of Kadillus Harbour on Piscina IV. Time and again, the greenskins used their numerical advantage to overrun the barricaded Dark Angels' positions, but with bolter and grenade, the Orks were driven back. When they ran out of ammunition, the Dark Angels used their boltguns as clubs, and though few survived, their heroic stand allowed reinforcements to arrive and secure ultimate victory.

ASSAULT SQUADS

As their name implies, Assault Squads are geared towards combat at close quarters. They are often unleashed in the first wave of an attack, racing to get to grips with the foe. Enemy infantry is assailed with chainsword and bolt pistol, while armoured vehicles are destroyed with krak grenades or melta bombs. It is the task of the Assault Squads to strike hard and fast, breaking through enemy weak points before turning rapidly onto their exposed and vulnerable flanks.

As they carry little in the way of ranged weaponry, it is pivotal for Assault Squads to close quickly with the enemy. To this end, they frequently employ jump packs – rocket-like thrusters worn on the back that allow their wearers to make powered jumps to advance quickly across a battlefield, leaping over obstacles and hurtling themselves over great distances. When wearing a jump pack, it is possible to deploy from airborne Thunderhawks, descending from the skies like vengeful Angels of Death. The Dark Angels use these sudden strikes to plunge deep into an opposing army, as they did to break Waaagh! Badrukk. It is also a useful way to bypass a foe's best-laid defences, as shown when they forced a breach in the Gothika Line during the siege against the Iron Warriors on Perditia. Such dangerous deployment can take a toll, and of all the Dark Angels squads, only the Ravenwing regularly sustains a higher casualty rate.

In many Chapters, Assault Squads are full of headstrong young Space Marines, freshly promoted from the Scout Squads. The Dark Angels are far more staid – their Assault Squads are not known for reckless charges or blood-curdling screams. Although Scouts are most likely to be promoted to the Assault Squads, none can leave the 10th Company before mastering the art of self-control. It would be a mistake to underestimate the ferocity of Dark Angels Assault Squads due to the stolid way in which they approach their missions, however. Above the thundering exhausts of jump packs and the angry buzz of chainswords can be heard sonorous chanting, a sound every bit as unnerving to a foe as battle cries or the howls of barbarous beasts. Those who have witnessed a Dark Angels Assault Squad in action never fail to remember the unsettling combination of the bloodthirsty and merciless rage with which they chop and blast apart their enemies, intermingled with their orderly hymnals – a deep chanting occasionally drowned out by screaming victims and the grinding sound of chainblades gouging through armour, flesh and bone.

DEVASTATOR SQUADS

Devastators are the most heavily armed of all Dark Angels squads. They bear a variety of heavy weapons with which to engage and destroy a foe's long-ranged weapons and blast apart any armoured vehicles. In addition to providing support to advancing Tactical or Assault Squads, a Devastator Squad is ideal for cracking open enemy fortifications and eliminating the most heavily armoured foes.

A Devastator Squad's weapon loadout might depend on the enemy, terrain or battlefield situation. The heavy bolter is a deadly anti-personnel weapon, while the missile launcher is useful for its triple role ability – able to fire krak missiles to penetrate armour, frag to blast away tightly packed foes, or flak missiles to target enemy flyers. The deadly plasma cannon is somewhat unstable, but can eradicate even the best protected enemies, while at close range, the multi-melta makes short work of bunkers or vehicles. For tank-busting at a distance, the lascannon is unmatched.

As per the Codex Astartes, not all members of the squad carry heavy weaponry. It is the Sergeant's job to lead and direct fire, and between one and four members in the squad will have a heavy weapon. The remainder are equipped with boltguns and grenades and tasked with providing close-fire support, although they are also used to spot targets for their more encumbered brethren. All those serving in the Devastator Squad, but particularly a squad's Veteran Sergeant, learn to appraise the lay of the land, able to pick out the best sites for firebases. A Devastator Squad is at its best when it can secure a vantage point from which to rain death upon the foe, before advancing to another firing position. Once entrenched upon an overlook, a Devastator Squad can dominate a battlefield – forcing the enemy to keep their heads down or be blown away – a situation that allows the Dark Angels to claim the initiative, with Tactical and Assault Squads eliminating the cowering foes.

There is a saying amongst Dark Angels, attributed to Lion El'Jonson himself, that is frequently used by Sergeants as they instruct their charges: 'Be slow to anger, quick to action'. The proper response is: 'The patient warrior knows that one well-placed shot can end a war'. It takes a steady hand to wait for a perfect shot, and to do so in the midst of battle takes all the training and discipline Devastator Squads can muster. They stand unflinching in the midst of incoming fire, until the right moment arises. Then, their weapons speak as one, unleashing death and destruction on the Emperor's foes.

	WS	BS	S	T	W	I	A	Ld	Sv
Space Marine	4	4	4	4	1	4	1	8	3+
Space Marine Sergeant	4	4	4	4	1	4	1	8	3+
Veteran Sergeant	4	4	4	4	1	4	2	9	3+

UNIT TYPE:
Tactical Squads and Devastator Squads: **Infantry.** Space Marine Sergeant and Veteran Sergeant are **Infantry (Character).**

Assault Squads: **Jump Infantry.** Space Marine Sergeant and Veteran Sergeant are **Jump Infantry (Character).**

WARGEAR:
Tactical Squads: **Power armour** (pg 65), **boltgun, bolt pistol, frag grenades, krak grenades.**

Assault Squads: **Power armour** (pg 65), **bolt pistol, chainsword, frag grenades, krak grenades, jump pack** (pg 63).

Devastator Squads: **Power armour** (pg 65), **boltgun, bolt pistol, frag grenades, krak grenades, signum** (Space Marine Sergeant and Veteran Sergeant only) (pg 64).

SPECIAL RULES: **And They Shall Know No Fear, Combat Squads** (pg 28), **Grim Resolve** (pg 28).

Company Veterans Squads

The Dark Angels are a solemn Chapter, not given to grandiose displays or acts of self-aggrandisement. Yet that is not to say that the Dark Angels do not reward heroism, or recognise their brethren who perform extreme deeds of bravery. After each engagement, as duty allows, those lost in battle are honoured in solemn ceremonies, as are those whose actions have merited such tribute.

To be acknowledged before the assembled might of the Dark Angels is both a proud and humbling moment – for each of the battle-brothers is, in their own right, a hero of many battles. Their leaders, cowled and robed, are living legends whose names are whispered in awe by even the most powerful men in the galaxy. In the wake of their mighty accomplishments, the greatest amongst the Dark Angels have left planets and whole star systems forever indebted by their deeds. To hear your name called out by such as them is one of the highest honours for a Dark Angel, for what could be better than to be praised by those who are themselves worthy of the highest praise?

Each battle company from the 3rd to the 9th has a cadre of Space Marines who have been honoured in this way, the finest warriors of their kind. At times of need, a company can gather such Dark Angels into a single unit, a powerful formation of Company Veterans. These formidable squads are deployed wherever the fighting is thickest and the need greatest. Such arrangements often last for just a single battle, although it is not unknown for these formations to stay together to achieve a particular long-term objective, or perhaps even to fight together throughout an entire campaign as a brotherhood of elite warriors.

The armouries of the Dark Angels are opened wide for Company Veterans so that, depending upon the requirements of their mission, they might arm themselves in any number of ways. Depending on need, a Veteran Squad could gear up entirely for close quarters fighting, load up on longer-ranged firepower or even equip themselves exclusively with plasma weaponry to negate the defences of heavily armoured foes.

Although they are honoured and held in high esteem, it is not always easy for outsiders to pick out the Chapter's honoured Veterans, for it is the nature of the Dark Angels to remain forever stoic and unembellished. Taking after the Company Masters, whom they revere as spiritual leaders as well as great tacticians, these Veterans renounce the garish and conspicuous – not for them the gold-encrusted armour of an honour guard or some ostentatious plume to denote to all onlookers their exalted station. Instead, only the keenest eye can perhaps discern a ceremonial robe or catch the odd gleam from some antiquated and honoured wargear gifted to them for their acts of bravery. On the battlefield, however, it is no hard task to mark out the Company Veterans – for they fight as a band of heroes, weapons blazing with precision bursts and foes falling before them like wheat before a scythe.

Those who manage to distinguish themselves still further while fighting within the Veteran Squads are soon considered for an even greater promotion. The mightiest warriors might be asked to join the elite ranks of the Command Squads or, if they are the types who excel at passing on the knowledge of their experience to others, they might rise to the rank of Sergeant. Only the most dedicated, those most excellent warriors to whom Chapter loyalty is all, will be asked to join the Inner Circle.

	WS	BS	S	T	W	I	A	Ld	Sv
Veteran	4	4	4	4	1	4	2	9	3+
Veteran Sergeant	4	4	4	4	1	4	2	9	3+

UNIT TYPE: **Infantry.**
Veteran Sergeant is **Infantry (Character).**

WARGEAR: **Power armour** (pg 65)**, boltgun, bolt pistol, frag grenades, krak grenades.**

SPECIAL RULES: **And They Shall Know No Fear, Combat Squads** (pg 28)**, Grim Resolve** (pg 28).

Scout Squads

The Dark Angels' history is replete with valiant actions performed by Space Marine Scouts. Not as heavily armoured as their more experienced brethren, Scouts are often deployed as light infantry or recon units – picking their way through enemy territory to unleash attacks upon vulnerable foes, or securing vital terrain in advance of the main army. It is in battle that Scouts truly absorb the most fundamental of tenets: that to be a Space Marine is to become death incarnate – regardless of situation, terrain or foe.

When newly initiated recruits, also called neophytes, are accepted into the Dark Angels, they first join the 10th Company as Space Marine Scouts. There, they are placed under the harsh tutelage of a Sergeant, a seasoned veteran rich in experience. It is his duty to lead the Scouts, oversee their training, and mould them into Mankind's greatest warriors. There is much to learn, and one critical step is to get a Scout accustomed to the many biologically engineered enhancements that have altered his body. He forgets his past life and learns what it means to be a Dark Angel. It is a new world of iron-hard discipline, endless drills, countless vows, and a total absorption of the catechisms of the Chapter.

A Scout progresses through separate stages of training, each marked by its own rites observed by the Scout Sergeant. Any neophytes found lacking are removed, destined to become Servitors, Chapter thralls, or simply never seen again. Before completing the first phase, recruits need to learn the Lore of the Lion and the Cant of the Combat Knife. They must be able to bolster themselves with the Litany of Battle and dozens more. By the fifth stage, they are neophytes no longer, and are welcomed into the ranks of the Space Marine Scouts in the Ceremony of Brotherhood.

By this time, a Scout has obtained, but not fully grown into, the might and constitution of a Space Marine – and he does not yet possess the martial skill that comes with practice and experience. The Scout's mind and body must be honed to think and react at inhuman speeds. Through drills, he has learned self-control and is able to fight through intense pain using mind chants. A Scout can stay alert beyond human endurance and will have become proficient with the battle gear upon which his life, and those of his battle-brothers, depend. The rituals to keep his equipment blessed and in good working order are second nature. Only at this point will the Scout Sergeant lead the Space Marine Scouts to battle.

Moving quickly and launching pinpoint strikes, Scouts are sent on a wide range of missions. One day might see Scouts at the forefront of a boarding action in the depths of space, while a subsequent battle could require investigating an enemy's advanced positions or launching a diversionary attack. Scouts typically fight as skirmishers, relying on their ability to move stealthily rather than advancing by brute force alone. Scouts can move noiselessly to infiltrate enemy positions, setting ambushes to disrupt their foe. Scouts are trained in all manner of weapons, trading their standard bolt pistols for long-ranged sniper rifles to exploit a high vantage point, or using shotguns in close confines. Only by dedicating himself wholly to his Chapter will a Scout ever be judged ready for promotion out of the 10th Company. Throughout their history, many of the greatest Dark Angels, including the Supreme Grand Master, have credited their years as Scouts, and the disciplined tutelage of their Scout Sergeants, as core to their great success.

	WS	BS	S	T	W	I	A	Ld	Sv
Scout	3	3	4	4	1	4	1	8	4+
Scout Sergeant	4	4	4	4	1	4	1	8	4+
Veteran Scout Sergeant	4	4	4	4	1	4	2	9	4+

UNIT TYPE: **Infantry.** Scout Sergeant and Veteran Scout Sergeant are **Infantry (Character).**

WARGEAR: **Scout armour** (pg 65), **boltgun, bolt pistol, frag grenades, krak grenades.**

SPECIAL RULES: **And They Shall Know No Fear, Combat Squads** (pg 28), **Infiltrate, Move Through Cover, Scouts.**

Dark Angels Tanks

The Dark Angels maintain a great variety of armoured transports and battle tanks in the vast arched bays within the Rock. Some vehicles are held by each Company, while others are allocated from the Chapter's armoury, where a cadre of Techmarines oversees and individually blesses every component of these sacred machines.

RHINOS

Rhino armoured personnel carriers are the mainstay transport of the Dark Angels. The Rhino is armed with a storm bolter, but its greatest strength is its durability in battle. Whether delivering Assault Squads into the fray or repositioning a Devastator Squad, the Rhino is fast and reliable.

The STC for the Rhino dates back to the Age of Technology and has changed little over the millennia. It is durable, easy to fix and has its own built-in self-repair system – useful on hostile battlefields. The Rhino can also be fitted out with a variety of upgrades, including one-shot, tank-busting hunter-killer missiles, obstacle-clearing dozer blades, or auxiliary armour plates. Also, the Rhino chassis serves as the basis for a wide range of battle tanks and weapons platforms, each with its own unique purpose on the battlefield.

		Armour			
	BS	F	S	R	HP
Rhino	4	11	11	10	3

UNIT TYPE: **Vehicle (Tank, Transport).**

WARGEAR: **Storm bolter, searchlight, smoke launchers.**

SPECIAL RULES:
Repair: If a Rhino is Immobilised, then in subsequent turns it may attempt to repair itself instead of shooting. To make the attempt, roll a D6 in the Shooting phase; on the roll of a 6, the vehicle is no longer Immobilised. Note that a successful Repair attempt does not restore a Hull Point.

TRANSPORT:
Transport Capacity: Ten models. It cannot carry models in Terminator armour.

Fire Points: Two models can fire from the Rhino's top hatch.

Access Points: The Rhino has one Access Point on each side of the hull and one at the rear.

RAZORBACKS

The Razorback trades some transport capacity for more destructive firepower, and is commonly deployed in a fire support role.

	BS	Armour F	Armour S	Armour R	HP
Razorback	4	11	11	10	3

UNIT TYPE: Vehicle (Tank, Transport).

WARGEAR: Twin-linked heavy bolter, searchlight, smoke launchers.

TRANSPORT:

Transport Capacity: Six models. It cannot carry models in Terminator armour.

Fire Points: None.

Access Points: The Razorback has one Access Point on each side of the hull and one at the rear.

'There is purity of purpose in the faith of the just.'

PREDATORS

The main battle tank of the Dark Angels is the Predator, with the Destructor and Annihilator patterns commonly seen.

	BS	Armour F	Armour S	Armour R	HP
Predator	4	13	11	10	3

UNIT TYPE: Vehicle (Tank).

WARGEAR: Autocannon, searchlight, smoke launchers.

VINDICATORS

The Vindicator is a siege tank that boasts the powerful demolisher cannon, a high-calibre weapon ideal for attacking foes in cover.

	BS	Armour F	Armour S	Armour R	HP
Vindicator	4	13	11	10	3

UNIT TYPE: Vehicle (Tank).

WARGEAR: **Demolisher cannon** (pg 60), **storm bolter, searchlight, smoke launchers.**

WHIRLWINDS

The Whirlwind, with its turret-mounted rack of missiles, is designed for long-ranged suppression of a foe.

	BS	Armour F	Armour S	Armour R	HP
Whirlwind	4	11	11	10	3

UNIT TYPE: Vehicle (Tank).

WARGEAR: Whirlwind multiple missile launcher (pg 61), **searchlight, smoke launchers.**

Land Raiders

The Land Raider is a mobile fortress, a heavily armoured and well armed fighting vehicle that is commonly deployed by the Dark Angels. With its ominously large frame, it appears as much like a well-protected bunker on tracks as an armoured vehicle, yet despite its bulk, a powerful engine allows the Land Raider to move with considerable speed.

Its mobility, combined with its adamantium armour and transport capacity, make the Land Raider a formidable assault vehicle, able to shrug off incoming fire while delivering its payload of warriors into the most dangerous part of the battlefield. However, the Land Raider is not merely a vehicle for ferrying troops – its frame bristles with weapons, typically mounting two God-hammer pattern twin-linked lascannons, making it superb at destroying enemy tanks, while twin-linked heavy bolters keep opposing infantry at bay. Over the millennia, different patterns of the Land Raider have been configured, and both the Crusader and the Redeemer designs have found their way into the standard arsenal of the Dark Angels.

Space Marines take great pride in their arms and armour, and Land Raiders, being amongst the largest and longest-serving vehicles, take a special place of honour amongst the Chapter's armaments. Each vehicle bears its Company markings, but such identification is not needed by the Dark Angels, who know each Land Raider by name and can identify vehicles by their sounds, silhouettes and battle-attributes alone. According to the Techmarines, who oversee vehicle repair and maintenance, the machine spirit of a Land Raider surpasses that of lesser machines – the Omnissiah's essence being especially well imbued in these mighty constructs.

DEATHWING VEHICLES

The most revered Land Raiders and Dreadnoughts in the Dark Angels army are those in the 1st Company. The hulls of these vehicles are painted bone white and the signs and marking of the Deathwing are upon them. These bone-coloured behemoths bestride the battlefield, bringing death to the foe.

Deathwing Vehicle: A Deathwing Vehicle has the Preferred Enemy (Chaos Space Marines) special rule, and if a Deathwing Vehicle suffers a penetrating hit, you can make your opponent re-roll the result on the Vehicle Damage table. You must accept the second roll, even if it is worse than the first.

LAND RAIDERS

		Armour			
	BS	F	S	R	HP
Land Raider	4	14	14	14	4

UNIT TYPE: Vehicle (Tank, Transport).

WARGEAR: Twin-linked heavy bolter, two twin-linked lascannons, searchlight, smoke launchers.

SPECIAL RULES:
Assault Vehicle,
Power of the Machine Spirit.

TRANSPORT:
Transport Capacity: Ten models.

Fire Points: None.

Access Points: A Land Raider has one Access Point on each side of the hull and one at the front.

'There is no substitute for a big gun.'

LAND RAIDER CRUSADERS

		Armour			
	BS	F	S	R	HP
Land Raider Crusader	4	14	14	14	4

UNIT TYPE: Vehicle (Tank, Transport).

WARGEAR: Twin-linked assault cannon, two hurricane bolters (pg 60), frag assault launcher (pg 65), searchlight, smoke launchers.

SPECIAL RULES:
Assault Vehicle,
Power of the Machine Spirit.

TRANSPORT:
Transport Capacity: Sixteen models.

Fire Points: None.

Access Points: A Land Raider Crusader has one Access Point on each side of the hull and one at the front.

'Understanding is not required, only submission.'

LAND RAIDER REDEEMERS

		Armour			
	BS	F	S	R	HP
Land Raider Redeemer	4	14	14	14	4

UNIT TYPE: Vehicle (Tank, Transport).

WARGEAR: Twin-linked assault cannon, two flamestorm cannons, frag assault launchers (pg 65), searchlight, smoke launchers.

SPECIAL RULES:
Assault Vehicle,
Power of the Machine Spirit.

TRANSPORT:
Transport Capacity: Twelve models.

Fire Points: None.

Access Points: A Land Raider Redeemer has one Access Point on each side of the hull and one at the front.

'Repent, for tomorrow you die.'

Drop Pods

Drop Pods hurtle through space at impossible speeds, ripping through low atmosphere and streaking towards the battlefield. They move at a velocity almost too fast for the eye to follow, only slowing when the retro-thrusters fire just before impact, allowing the Drop Pod to land rather than crash. The air fills with dust clouds kicked up by the landing, and the still-glowing hull barely comes to rest before the hatches blow clear and the occupants disembark – emerging into the fray with guns blazing.

Drop Pods are launched from spaceships in low orbit – in some ways resembling emergency escape pods. Using powerful thrusters to correct their descent, Drop Pods speed towards their targeted drop zone. Outside, the hull radiates with the incandescent heat of atmospheric re-entry. Nestled inside each well-armoured cocoon of ceramite and plasteel can be found a Space Marine squad or Dreadnought. Dimly lit by the blue-green tinge of control panels, there is little room inside a Drop Pod for anything but its occupants, all of whom must be firmly strapped into position, for it is a turbulent ride. So fierce is the downwards plummet that any without the superhuman constitution of a Space Marine would suffer a painful death – the gravitational pressures alone would collapse a man's insides, to say nothing of the bone-breaking turbulence the craft endures as it speeds towards the planet. All are quiet during descent, despite the trauma. For the Dark Angels this is a time for reflection, the silence only broken by hymnals of vengeance or the chanting of battle mantras, as the warriors steel themselves for the bloodshed that awaits.

For those who know anything of Space Marine operations, the concept of a Drop Pod Assault is widely known: however, to experience such a thing in person is entirely different. Nothing can prepare a foe for the cracking boom of the sound barrier, which alerts those in the vicinity of the landing. Those fast enough to turn can just catch the screaming descent of the shape streaking from the skies before the roaring glare of the retro-thrusters begins. Even before the reality of the situation registers, comes the sudden shock of the Emperor's Finest bursting forth and sweeping all before them. Terrible and swift; it is truly as if Angels of Death themselves have arrived from the heavens.

		Armour			
	BS	F	S	R	HP
Drop Pod	4	12	12	12	3

UNIT TYPE: **Vehicle (Open-topped, Transport).**

WARGEAR: **Storm bolter.**

SPECIAL RULES:

Drop Pod Assault: Drop Pods must enter play using the Deep Strike rules. At the beginning of your first turn, choose half of your Drop Pods (rounding up) to make a 'Drop Pod Assault'. Units making a Drop Pod Assault arrive on their controlling player's first turn. The arrival of the remaining Drop Pods is rolled for as normal. A unit that Deep Strikes via Drop Pod cannot charge in the turn it arrives.

Immobile: A Drop Pod cannot move once it has entered the battle, and counts in all respects as a vehicle that has suffered an Immobilised damage result that cannot be repaired in any way.

Inertial Guidance System: Should a Drop Pod scatter on top of impassable terrain or another model (friend or foe) then reduce the scatter distance by the minimum required in order to avoid the obstacle. Note that if a Drop Pod scatters off the edge of the board then they will suffer a Deep Strike Mishap as per the *Warhammer 40,000* rulebook.

TRANSPORT:

Transport Capacity: Ten models or one Dreadnought.

Once the Drop Pod has landed, the hatches are blown and all passengers must immediately disembark. Once passengers have disembarked, no models can embark on the Drop Pod for the remainder of the game.

Dreadnoughts

Dreadnoughts are massive fighting machines that bristle with weaponry. They stride the battlefield seeking to smash foes, as incoming enemy fire patters harmlessly from their thick ceramite hulls. More than just devastating engines of war, Dreadnoughts are the living embodiment of a Chapter's spirit, and walking pieces of its history.

Unlike other vehicles, Dreadnoughts are not crewed, for once a pilot is interred inside, he can never again step forth. For this reason, only critically injured Space Marines are so enshrined, granted a living entombment to continue serving the Chapter. Only the most dedicated are considered for the honour of being interred into a Dreadnought, and even in their death throes they must prove to be of sound mind.

Many years might pass before a candidate for transferral into the armoured sarcophagus of a Dreadnought is presented. The Techmarines must hardwire the crippled hero into the fighting machine before his consciousness dims for all time. He must be spliced into the Dreadnought, bound by electro-fibre implants and linked so that nerves and mechanical senses become one. Only the strongest-willed survive the process. To the Techmarines, the procedures are holy rituals, and care is taken until the innermost chamber is locked and filled with amniotic fluids. Upon completion, the Space Marine can move, hear and speak with his new mechanical body. The fallen warrior's intelligence, memories and fighting prowess live on – now encased within a walking bunker.

Powerful servo-motors drive the Dreadnought, its armoured hulk and ability to fire on the move making it ideal at leading assaults or a perfect bulwark for any defensive formation. A variety of weapon fits are available – the close support pattern of assault cannon and power fist is the most common configuration, but the tank-hunting lascannon or fortification-clearing heavy flamer are regularly employed. The worth of a Dreadnought is greater than its battlefield role alone, however, as many have seen much of the galaxy and fought against countless enemies. Deep in the under-armouries of the Rock, there are Dreadnoughts who have served the Dark Angels since the Age of the Forging.

Should a Dreadnought fall in battle, the Chapter will do their utmost to retrieve both the machine and its contents. With much honour and reverence, they will finally lay to rest the Dreadnought's occupant, so that the massive armoured shell might be repaired to once again house a dying hero. Although incredibly protected and preserved, even a Space Marine cocooned within a Dreadnought does not live forever.

VENERABLE DREADNOUGHTS

Some longest serving Dreadnoughts are crewed by Dark Angels who served with the First Company and they still bear the bone white armour of the Deathwing. These Venerable Dreadnoughts have borne witness to the Chapter's secret hunt and members of the Inner Circle still seek their advice. It is difficult to rouse the eldest of the machines, and many legends slumber in the Halls of Silence, powered down between actions and awoken only in dire need.

				Armour					
	WS	BS	S	F	S	R	I	A	HP
Dreadnought	4	4	6	12	12	10	4	2	3
Venerable Dreadnought	5	5	6	12	12	10	4	2	3

UNIT TYPE: **Vehicle (Walker).**

WARGEAR: **Power fist with built-in storm bolter, multi-melta, searchlight, smoke launchers.**

SPECIAL RULES: **Deathwing Vehicle** (Venerable Dreadnought only) (pg 40).

The Deathwing

The Deathwing is the 1st Company of the Dark Angels and they rank amongst the greatest of all fighting units within the Imperium. Across the cosmos, there are hundreds of planets where legends are told, tales of the bone white Terminators of the Deathwing performing some epic deed. It took only three squads of Deathwing Terminators to break the back of the Pontus rebellion, cleansing an entire hive-city in the process. While dozens of other Space Marine Chapters had failed to contain the system-spanning Waaagh! of Warboss Gruskull, it took only a lone Deathwing Knights squad to end the threat by slaughtering the Ork leader and his hundred-strong bodyguard.

The Dark Angels' 1st Company is made up of veterans and broken into three distinct units: Terminator Squads, Command Squads and Knights. All are elites entirely outfitted in Terminator armour, a luxury few Chapters can match. Officially known as Tactical Dreadnought armour, a Terminator suit is the heaviest protection a Dark Angel can wear, short of being entombed within a Dreadnought. Terminators are sent on the most desperate missions: boarding infested space hulks, crossing no-man's land, or attacking the most horrific enemies – Greater Daemons, xenos monstrosities and earth-shaking daemon engines.

Initiation into the Deathwing is not just an honour for the Chapter's best warriors – it is a commencement into the first level of the hidden order of the Dark Angels. Upon entering, some of the Chapter's secrets are revealed, and a Dark Angel learns of Luther's betrayal and the hunt for the Fallen. This epiphany brings full understanding of the Chapter's apocryphal stories and sets out the truth behind the mission to hunt down and destroy the Fallen Dark Angels, no matter how long it takes, or what the cost. Most Dark Angels strike forces will include a Deathwing Terminator Squad or two, although on occasion the Company has deployed en masse – a cataclysmic event, as seen at the siege of Dominus Prime, or during the Hrakon campaign.

DEATHWING TERMINATOR SQUADS

The bulk of the 1st Company is composed of Terminator Squads, indefatigable warriors who blast apart their enemies with storm bolters while advancing into assault range. Deathwing Terminators feature a mix of weaponry, for both long-ranged and close combat orientated roles. Terminators typically begin engagements aboard an orbiting starship, teleporting to the battlefield at a prearranged time, often homing in on a signal from ranging Ravenwing units. By the time foes see the flash signifying their arrival, it is too late. The Deathwing appear in a blazing hail of gunfire, as if they had begun firing while en route. They live up to their name, arriving like a sword stroke to deliver the deathblow.

	WS	BS	S	T	W	I	A	Ld	Sv
Deathwing Terminator	4	4	4	4	1	4	2	9	2+
Deathwing Term. Sgt.	4	4	4	4	1	4	2	9	2+

UNIT TYPE: **Infantry.** Deathwing Terminator Sergeant is **Infantry (Character).**

WARGEAR: **Terminator armour** (pg 65), **storm bolter, power fist** (Deathwing Terminator only), **power sword** (Deathwing Sergeant only).

SPECIAL RULES: **Inner Circle** (pg 28), **Split Fire.**

Deathwing Assault: Units entirely composed of models that have both this special rule and Terminator armour can choose to make a Deathwing Assault. Immediately after determining Warlord Traits, tell your opponent which units are making a Deathwing Assault, and make a secret note of whether it takes place during your first or second turn. All units making the Deathwing Assault automatically arrive via Deep Strike at the start of the chosen turn – there is no need to roll for reserves.

Vengeful Strike: When a model with this special rule arrives by Deep Strike, it treats all of its ranged weapons (not including psychic powers) as having the Twin-linked special rule until the end of the turn.

DEATHWING COMMAND SQUADS

The highest-ranking members of the Inner Circle are sometimes accompanied by a Command Squad from the 1st Company. Such a hand-picked formation of the most veteran Deathwing Terminators makes a formidable unit, ideal for a bodyguard or to be assigned special duties by a Librarian or Interrogator-Chaplain. They can be equipped for any role and often include specialists such as standard bearers, Apothecaries or even the Company's Champion. Belial, the Grand Master of the Deathwing, has personally led many a Command Squad straight into the heart of battle, forging a breach in enemy lines and crushing opposing leaders.

	WS	BS	S	T	W	I	A	Ld	Sv
Deathwing Terminator	4	4	4	4	1	4	2	9	2+
Deathwing Apothecary	4	4	4	4	1	4	2	9	2+
Deathwing Champion	5	4	4	4	1	4	2	9	2+

UNIT TYPE: **Infantry.** Deathwing Apothecary and Deathwing Champion are **Infantry (Character).**

WARGEAR:

Deathwing Terminator: **Terminator armour** (pg 65), **storm bolter, power fist.**

Deathwing Apothecary: **Terminator armour** (pg 65), **storm bolter, narthecium** (pg 63).

Deathwing Champion: **Terminator armour** (pg 65), **Halberd of Caliban** (pg 62).

SPECIAL RULES: **Deathwing Assault** (pg 44), **Inner Circle** (pg 28), **Split Fire, Vengeful Strike** (pg 44).

DEATHWING KNIGHTS

Deathwing Knights are an imposing sight, for in them lives on some semblance of the Lion himself; they too embody silent strength and a veiled, yet palpable nobility. In the stratified circles of the Dark Angels, the Deathwing Knights are the pinnacle within an elite – only the Masters are of greater rank within the Chapter, and they are chosen only from within the stern order of Knights. None but the most fell-handed of warriors from the 1st Company are promoted into the Inner Circle of the Deathwing, and displaying might in battle is not enough to be so knighted. A warrior must be wholly dedicated to the Chapter, and must show an obsession with the secret crusade to hunt the Fallen.

When a member of the Deathwing is deemed worthy, he is brought into the Chamber of Judgments to face a series of challenges, each individualised to test his strength, resolve and loyalty to the Chapter past any breaking point he may have. Should he prevail, the warrior is granted the title of Knight and passes beneath the shadowed arch. The Watchers in the Dark present to him a mace of absolution and a storm shield – heirlooms of the Great Crusade, with powers beyond even the warriors who bear them. In battle, the Deathwing Knights are a heavy shock force – teleporting to the fight with shields locked. With incoming fire ricocheting off them, the Knights march for the greatest threat with impunity, first slamming into them with their mighty storm shields, before setting about the foe with their maces and flails. In the presence of a heretic, the Knights power up their ancient weapons to deliver a killing blow of earth-shattering magnitude.

	WS	BS	S	T	W	I	A	Ld	Sv
Deathwing Knight	5	4	4	4	1	4	2	9	2+
Knight Master	5	4	4	4	1	4	3	9	2+

UNIT TYPE: **Infantry.** Knight Master is **Infantry (Character).**

WARGEAR: **Terminator armour** (pg 65), **mace of absolution** (Deathwing Knight only) (pg 62), **flail of the Unforgiven** (Knight Master only) (pg 62), **storm shield** (pg 64).

SPECIAL RULES: **Deathwing Assault** (pg 44), **Hammer of Wrath, Inner Circle** (pg 28).

Fortress of Shields: Any model with the Inner Circle special rule that is in base contact with two or more models with this special rule has +1 Toughness. With careful positioning, this can increase the whole squad's Toughness.

You Cannot Hide: Models with this special rule that are attacking with a Melee weapon score a Precision Strike on a To Hit roll of 6, in the same manner as characters.

THE RAVENWING

For speed, audacity and the ability to launch lightning attacks, the Ravenwing – the Dark Angels 2nd Company – have earned a reputation that is second to none. They are not formed up as per a Codex Astartes-compliant battle company, but instead are organised entirely into fast, hard-hitting elements that are as unique as they are effective.

All members of the Ravenwing operate a fast vehicle, be it a Space Marine bike, Attack Bike, one of the many variants of Land Speeder or perhaps an atmospheric fighter. They typically work together in mixed formations: the standard ten-strong squad within the Ravenwing is the Attack Squadron, a force made up of six brethren riding Space Marine bikes, two riding an Attack Bike, and two crewing a Land Speeder. These are further supported by additional Land Speeders or squads of the veteran bike-mounted warriors known as Black Knights. All are optimised for speed and mobility over firepower or the ability to sustain assaults.

As they streak into battle, Ravenwing Attack Squadrons often break into their disparate parts. Weaving in and out of each others' paths, each element works with the synchronicity of thousands of drills and the experience garnered upon blood-soaked battlefields across the Imperium. With but a signal flashed across the comm-net, the different elements will break off at speed to pursue their own goals up and down the enemy lines, only to reconverge moments later to focus their destructive powers upon on a single target.

As the Ravenwing range ahead of the main force, they are often the first to find and engage a foe. This is their specialty, as the Ravenwing are the black-clad huntsmen of the Dark Angels – and they are tasked with seeking out and pinning down the foe until the rest of the Chapter arrives. While the entire 2nd Company is occasionally deployed in a single action, most often the Ravenwing is broken into its component squads and attached to work alongside Dark Angels strike forces spread across the galaxy.

RAVENWING BIKERS

Bikers form over half of the 2nd Company's bulk and they are the centre of any Ravenwing attack. The Space Marine bikes lay down a torrent of fire from twin-linked bolters and accelerate into combat should a vulnerable target reveal itself. It is Ravenwing doctrine to avoid becoming bogged down, where their speed is negated and the enemy's superior numbers can be brought to bear. Thus, the

Ravenwing Bikers might charge into a foe, but unless they break them immediately, the bikers are likely to streak off, leaving their foe bewildered, unsure of which direction the next attack will come from. Equipped with teleportation homers, Ravenwing bikes often drive deep into the heart of their quarry before summoning the Deathwing. The Ravenwing ride down any who attempt to flee, mercilessly allowing none to escape the ensuing massacre.

The Attack Bike augments the more lightly armed Ravenwing bikes, lending its heavier firepower where needed. The Attack Bike is ideal for getting into position to support the Ravenwing's assaults, clearing the path ahead of the onrushing bikes with its heavy bolter. Some Attack Bikes are outfitted with a multi-melta: these are tasked with hunting down and destroying enemy armour which would otherwise endanger their brethren.

	WS	BS	S	T	W	I	A	Ld	Sv
Ravenwing Biker	4	4	4	5	1	4	1	8	3+
Ravenwing Sergeant	4	4	4	5	1	4	1	8	3+
Ravenwing Veteran Sgt.	4	4	4	5	1	4	2	9	3+
Ravenwing Attack Bike	4	4	4	5	2	4	2	8	3+

UNIT TYPE: **Bike.** Ravenwing Sergeant and Ravenwing Veteran Sergeant are **Bike (Character).**

WARGEAR: **Power armour** (pg 65), **bolt pistol, twin-linked boltgun, heavy bolter** (Attack Bike only), **frag grenades, krak grenades, teleport homer** (pg 64).

SPECIAL RULES: **And They Shall Know No Fear, Grim Resolve** (pg 28), **Hit & Run, Scouts.**

Ravenwing Combat Squad: The squadron's Attack Bike and Land Speeder are purchased together with the squadron's bikes, but from then on they always operate as completely independent units of one model. If a Ravenwing Attack Squadron consists of six Ravenwing Bikers (including a Sergeant but excluding an Attack Bike) then it may break down into two Combat Squads of three Ravenwing Bikers following the rules for Combat Squads (pg 28).

RAVENWING BLACK KNIGHTS

Those who survive in the Ravenwing long enough learn to take mobile warfare to the next level. If they can pass the Seven Rites of the Raven, they will be inducted into the Black Knights, the Inner Circle of the 2nd Company. There, they will learn the real reason behind their hunt.

Black Knights ride to battle atop Mark IV Raven-pattern Space Marine bikes, powerful machines outfitted with deadly plasma talons. To signify their rank, they carry corvus hammers, which are modelled after an ancient Caliban monster-hunting weapon. Their riding skills are supreme, and they can drive at top speed through impediments to close with a foe. On their approach, their plasma talons tear holes in the enemy lines before they ride over their quarry, cracking armour and sundering flesh with their hammers as they go. Against more formidable opponents, those Black Knights trained in the use of the Ravenwing grenade launcher fire a salvo of specialised rad and stasis shells, which can make even the hardest of enemy units more vulnerable to a sustained assault.

	WS	BS	S	T	W	I	A	Ld	Sv
Ravenwing Black Knight	4	4	4	5	1	4	2	9	3+
Ravenwing Huntmaster	4	4	4	5	1	4	2	9	3+

UNIT TYPE: **Bike.**
Ravenwing Huntmaster is **Bike (Character).**

WARGEAR: **Power armour** (pg 65), **bolt pistol, plasma talon** (pg 60), **corvus hammer** (pg 62), **frag grenades, krak grenades, teleport homer** (pg 64).

SPECIAL RULES: **And They Shall Know No Fear, Grim Resolve** (pg 28), **Hit & Run, Scouts, Skilled Rider.**

RAVENWING COMMAND SQUADS

Bike-mounted Command Squads consist of experienced Ravenwing Black Knights who form a swift bodyguard around a mounted officer, or execute other specialised missions. These squads usually include several Chapter specialists – an Apothecary to tend to the wounded on far-flung scouting missions, a standard bearer, and the Ravenwing Company Champion wielding a deadly blade of Caliban.

When a Ravenwing Command Squad rides to battle, they form a rallying point for one of the most fearsome fast strike forces in the galaxy. Beneath the shadow of their fluttering standard, the black-armoured warriors of the Ravenwing bring death to the foe.

	WS	BS	S	T	W	I	A	Ld	Sv
Ravenwing Black Knight	4	4	4	5	1	4	2	9	3+
Ravenwing Apothecary	4	4	4	5	1	4	2	9	3+
Ravenwing Champion	5	4	4	5	1	4	2	9	3+

UNIT TYPE: **Bike.** Ravenwing Apothecary and Ravenwing Champion are **Bike (Character).**

WARGEAR:
Ravenwing Black Knight: **Power armour** (pg 65), **bolt pistol, plasma talon** (pg 60), **corvus hammer** (pg 62), **frag grenades, krak grenades, teleport homer** (pg 64).

Ravenwing Apothecary: **Power armour** (pg 65), **plasma talon** (pg 60), **corvus hammer** (pg 62), **frag grenades, krak grenades, narthecium** (pg 63), **teleport homer** (pg 64).

Ravenwing Champion: **Power armour** (pg 65), **bolt pistol, plasma talon** (pg 60), **blade of Caliban** (pg 62), **frag grenades, krak grenades, teleport homer** (pg 64).

SPECIAL RULES: **And They Shall Know No Fear, Grim Resolve** (pg 28), **Hit & Run, Scouts, Skilled Rider.**

Ravenwing Land Speeders

If bike-mounted Space Marines form the mainstay of the Ravenwing, then Land Speeders provide the bulk of the 2nd Company's heavier firepower. With their repulsion plates and inverse gravity field, the Land Speeders are able to skim a planet's surface, boosting above terrain or rapidly descending from a Thunderhawk Gunship as it strafes overhead. In the Ravenwing's unconventional composition, a single Land Speeder makes up part of the standard Attack Squadron, while others (up to five) are grouped into Support Squadrons that can be split as needed. This unusual doctrine has been developed because the Ravenwing use Land Speeders to perform a variety of battlefield roles, due to their versatile weapons loadout. The Dark Angels can equip their Land Speeders for light probing reconnaissance, advanced scouting, tank-hunting, seek and destroy missions, and so on.

LAND SPEEDERS

Most often, Land Speeders form highly mobile support for the ground-bound bike elements of the Ravenwing or larger Dark Angels strike forces. While part of the Ravenwing closes with the enemy, it is the Land Speeders that ensure that the bike-mounted spearhead can reach its quarry. To do this requires vehicles and pilots as mobile and quick-witted as the bike formations themselves. The Ravenwing advocate a fluid style of attack, and all its members must be ready to switch from well-rehearsed set-piece attacks to improvised breakthroughs or rapid pursuit of fleeing foes. On Straton, during the battles of the Third Tyrannic War, Land Speeder Typhoons worked in unison to lay down a missile barrage that blasted a lane through the swarming Tyranid creatures, allowing Space Marine bikes to penetrate deep into the enemy's centre, where they called in the Deathwing to destroy the synapse creatures providing purpose to the xenos assault. In the brutal cityfighting on the toxic world of Sephlagm, Land Speeder Tornados mounting heavy flamers cleared the streets, allowing the Black Knights access straight to the rebels' base, where they quickly dispatched the heretical leaders.

		Armour			
	BS	F	S	R	HP
Land Speeder	4	10	10	10	2

UNIT TYPE: **Vehicle (Fast, Skimmer).**

WARGEAR: **Heavy bolter.**

SPECIAL RULES: **Deep Strike.**

LAND SPEEDER VENGEANCE

The Ravenwing have always sought more firepower to support their hard-hitting attacks. An answer to this quest came in M36, with the discovery of the STC for a strange type of Land Speeder. Its larger chassis and superior lift-engines could house heavy weaponry, allowing it to mount the plasma storm battery – a relic weapon long held in the the Rock's armoury. Thus was born the Land Speeder Vengeance, a strike vehicle exclusively employed by the Unforgiven Chapters.

In conjunction with the Land Speeders of the Support Squadron, the Land Speeder Vengeance has proven its worth on the battlefield time and again, able to keep pace with the fastest of the Ravenwing vehicles and able to deliver devastating volleys from its deadly plasma storm battery.

		Armour			
	BS	F	S	R	HP
Land Speeder Vengeance	4	10	10	10	2

UNIT TYPE: **Vehicle (Fast, Skimmer).**

WARGEAR: **Heavy bolter, plasma storm battery** (pg 60).

SPECIAL RULES: **Deep Strike.**

RAVENWING DARKSHROUDS

At the centre of a rippling cloud of gloom, the Ravenwing Darkshroud drifts forwards, a partially seen force field of haze emanating outwards from the ancient reliquary it holds aloft. Of all the archaic relics deployed on the field of battle by the Unforgiven, the Darkshroud is perhaps the strangest. Those who have witnessed it at close range and felt its caliginous pall, and lived to tell of it, are disturbed for ever more. Although a bane to their foes, the Darkshroud is a powerful icon of the Chapter and the Dark Angels will protect it with their lives.

How such a device came to be is a tale that began long ago. When the planet of Caliban was engulfed by a Warp storm it was split asunder, yet not all was destroyed or consumed. Protected by an ancient force field of prodigious strength, the fortress monastery of the Dark Angels, and much of the bedrock upon which it stood, was saved. The collision of that storm with the indestructible force field, however, had many repercussions. That some contaminant leaked within the shield's perimeter is a given, for the false atmosphere within the domed field that surrounds the Rock is, to this day, still crowned with chain lightnings, and darksome squalls waft across its wasted surface.

Early in that catastrophic tumult, the Tower of Angels – the proud citadel that topped the largest fortress monastery of the Order and subsequently the Dark Angels – had fallen in ruin. Although the Dark Angels would take the barren remnants of their homeworld as a base, they have never attempted to rebuild that wreckage above. Standing proud amongst the desolate rubble, however, the Dark Angels did find some elements of their old fortress citadel that withstood the collision of unstoppable force with impenetrable shield. Amidst the debris there stood statues – carved figures from a past age, old even for Caliban. Those stone eyes had seen all of the tragedies that had befallen the Emperor's First Legion and they now glowed with mysterious power, imbued with the energies released on that fateful day.

The Stone Guardians, or Ten Brothers of the Order, as they were known, were taken below into the Rock and locked in stasis displays deep in the Reclusiam for years. It wasn't until the desperation of the Vendetta Campaign that the Dark Angels at last felt compelled to unleash their arcane power upon the battlefield. Each statue was mounted upon the chassis of a Land Speeder Vengeance, with great cables siphoning off its strange energy and amplifying it, and a power field of unknown quality rippled outwards from this grim, new Dark Angels reliquary.

In battle, the Darkshroud is used in support of the Ravenwing, its otherworldly veil serving to partially obscure and protect the bikes and light vehicles as they streak towards the foe. Even the blazing beam of a lascannon can be swallowed within that gloaming field of eldritch power, dissipating harmlessly while the Ravenwing speed onwards.

With a Darkshroud as a foreboding escort, units of Black Knights and Ravenwing Attack Squadrons can rev their engines and hurtle straight into an enemy gun line with impunity, protected from the foe's firepower as if by the Emperor's own blessing.

	BS	Armour F	Armour S	Armour R	HP
Ravenwing Darkshroud	4	10	10	10	2

UNIT TYPE: **Vehicle (Fast, Skimmer).**

WARGEAR: **Heavy bolter.**

SPECIAL RULES: **Deep Strike, Scouts.**

Icon of Old Caliban: The presence of Darkshrouds inspires nearby Dark Angels to greater acts of valour. When determining assault results, friendly Dark Angels units add +1 to their total if there are one or more Ravenwing Darkshrouds within 12".

Shroud of Angels: The Ravenwing Darkshroud has the Shrouded special rule. In addition, all friendly units within 6" of one or more Ravenwing Darkshrouds gain the Stealth special rule (this does not affect the Darkshrouds themselves).

Nephilim Jetfighters

Sleek Ravenwing aircraft are deployed from the fighter bays on either the Rock or any of the Dark Angels' Strike Cruisers. Although sometimes given the task of escorting Thunderhawks to their drop sites, the main role for the Nephilim is as an interceptor to establish air superiority over the battlefield, allowing their brethren to concentrate on ground targets with little concern for aerial assault.

To pilot such swift attack craft, the Dark Angels have naturally turned to the Ravenwing – for the 2nd Company cultivates the skills needed for such rapid manoeuvres. Ever since its founding, all members of the Ravenwing have been trained to pilot any of the vehicles their company utilises in battle; however, it is the oversized 2nd and 3rd squads that have traditionally served as the front line pilots. On the whole, the Dark Angels exhibit conservatism regarding their wargear, preferring the standard-issue weapons and vehicles that have served the Chapter for thousands of years. Ravenwing pilots, however, do not show such obstinacy. While they revere the ancient relics that have been used in combat since the days of the Great Crusade, they continually push the Techmarines for enhancements, modifications or newer craft – anything that can boost the speed with which they can take the fight to those who would deny the Emperor's will.

The Nephilim Jetfighters have only been used by the Dark Angels since late M40, when the Standard Template Construct for the improved engines was discovered while hunting a suspected Fallen, Baelor the Imposter, in the Nephilim Sector. Designated the Lionheart engine, the technology was used to modify older designs, though many features were left in place to appease the machine-spirits. The end product was a more agile fighter with improved speed, even while carrying more powerful armaments. With a twin-linked lascannon mounted in its nose, the Nephilim is ideally suited to bringing down aerial targets. It has proven itself on innumerable occasions, perhaps most notably during the Piscina IV battle, when a trio of Nephilim Jetfighters were, between them, able to shoot down over four-dozen Ork aircraft. By keeping the skies clear of foes, they allowed the Dark Angels and the planetary defence force on the ground to hold out against the greenskins' superior numbers.

Given their speed, and the skill of their pilots, it was only a matter of time before the Nephilim Jetfighters were called upon in battle. In 146.M41, a Ravenwing formation was tasked with a special reconnaissance mission during the massive tank battles fought between the Imperial Guard and Eldar on the world of Kundra. After pressing deep into enemy territory, the Ravenwing Attack Squadrons found their role reversed; they were being stalked and encircled by a host of mobile grav-tanks. Unable to successfully confront so much enemy armour, the Ravenwing requested assistance from their skyborne brothers. Sweeping out of the eternal twilight of that cursed world, the Nephilim Jetfighters were more than capable in an anti-tank role. Those craft outfitted with avenger mega bolters proved effective at raking through entire squadrons of xenos jetbikes, while those equipped with lascannons destroyed the heavier grav-vehicles. The skies were turned black with the fell contrails of the Nephilims' missiles, and the Eldar were routed. Since that day, the Dark Angels have known that – whatever the situation, whatever the foe – the sleek Nephilim will guard the skies above them, and the angels rule the heavens.

		Armour			
	BS	**F**	**S**	**R**	**HP**
Nephilim Jetfighter	4	11	11	11	3

UNIT TYPE: **Vehicle (Flyer).**

WARGEAR: **Twin-linked heavy bolter, twin-linked lascannon, six blacksword missiles** (pg 60).

SPECIAL RULES: **Strafing Run.**

Unrelenting Hunter: When shooting at enemy vehicles, a Nephilim Jetfighter can choose to treat any Weapon Destroyed results as Immobilised results.

Ravenwing Dark Talons

The Dark Talon is perhaps the deadliest weapon in the Ravenwing's armoury, and it plays a pivotal role in the 2nd Company's eternal hunt. It is a strange and ominous-looking craft, an atmospheric fighter topped with sepulchre-like spires and half-covered in a gothic façade. Those who have faced the Dark Angels and seen the menacing attack run of this craft have learned to fear its distinctive silhouette, knowing that the Ravenwing Dark Talon is flying death – a grim reaper of the skies.

The Dark Talon flies low, following the contours of the surrounding terrain. By hitting its ground-facing boost jets, the Dark Talon can literally hang in the air – hovering above its victim like some black bird of prey. Upon spotting a target, the Dark Talon is equipped to attack in two ways. It is armed for direct support to allies on the ground; underslung on each of its blunt wings is a racked hurricane bolter, allowing it to pour out a prodigious amount of firepower that can mow down lightly armoured enemy troops like a scythe cutting wheat. The Dark Talon also carries a single bomb, and should the situation be right, it will accelerate on a bombing run, delivering its strange payload to the marked quarry.

The Dark Talon does not just drop ordnance; it delivers an archaic holdover from the Age of Technology. The weapon carried in the belly of each Dark Talon is an archaic stasis bomb. In the workshops deep in the Rock, the Techmarines labour lovingly over the construction of each bomb, using an STC template they have repeatedly denied owning. The blast of a stasis bomb causes a degree of damage but, more importantly, will momentarily halt the flow of time. While the actual time-stoppage is measured in mere milliseconds, this unnatural disruption to the time stream has lingering effects on those in close proximity to such a blast, causing gut-wrenching disorientation and slowing their reaction times. The victims of a stasis bomb are ripe to be finished off by nearby squads; typically these are Ravenwing Attack Squadrons or Deathwing Terminators.

Situated in the nose of the craft is the Dark Talon's most awe-inspiring weapon. The rift cannon, sometimes referred to as the stained glass cannon, is a weapon developed at the zenith of Mankind's technological achievements and his hubris. The Chapter's Techmarines cannot fathom the secrets of its construction, and it strains their knowledge to keep its machine-spirits docile. However, their rituals of maintenance preserve its function so that when the weapon fires, it emits a beam of scintillating colours that explode into a blossom of oblivion. Such is the power of its shot that it cracks reality, its blast consuming those too near to the rift, while those who survive the brief tear in realspace find themselves thrown awry by close proximity to such an unnatural phenomenon.

In addition to its mighty arsenal, the Dark Talon carries a stasis-crypt holding cell. It is into these awful confines that Dark Angels' captives are loaded so that they might be ferried up to the orbital fleet and, ultimately, to the dungeons of the Rock and the attentions of the awaiting Interrogator-Chaplains. The Fallen fear this fate more than any other, for that last ascension leads not to redemption, but only to great pain and death.

	BS	Armour F	Armour S	Armour R	HP
Dark Talon	4	11	11	11	3

UNIT TYPE: **Vehicle (Flyer).**

WARGEAR: **Two hurricane bolters** (pg 60), **rift cannon** (pg 61), **stasis bomb** (pg 61).

SPECIAL RULES:

Hover Strike: At the start of its Movement phase, a model with this special rule can declare that it is making a special Hover Strike this turn. If it does so, its unit type changes to Skimmer until the start of its next Movement phase. It gains the Strafing Run special rule but cannot move, except to pivot on the spot.

AZRAEL

SUPREME GRAND MASTER OF THE DARK ANGELS, KEEPER OF THE TRUTH

Commander Azrael is the present, and some would say greatest, Supreme Grand Master of the Dark Angels. In a close-mouthed Chapter that eschews self-aggrandisement, the martial respect and deference paid to Azrael speaks volumes – and in the wider Imperium, even a secretive and monastic nature cannot dim the glow of the heroic deeds performed by Azrael and his heralded Chapter.

While Azrael's complete tale remains hidden within the undisclosed Chapter records, some details of his rapid rise through the ranks are known. Azrael's beginnings are a mystery, although rumours persist that he was inducted into the Chapter from the wild, head-hunting tribesmen of the feral planet of Kimmeria, a known Dark Angels recruiting world. Whatever his background, like all Dark Angels he foreswore his past for a life of service to the Chapter.

Azrael was appointed to the Deathwing and later became the Master of the 3rd Company, before being named as the Grand Master of the Deathwing in 917.M41. From there, he famously led the assault that slew the Daemon-possessed planetary governor of Sephlagm, claiming vengeance for the Imperium before the order for Exterminatus removed the befouled planet from the heavens. Upon the death of Supreme Grand Master Naberius during the Rhamiel Betrayal in 939.M41, Azrael was named as his successor. Since that time, Azrael has distinguished himself, and his Chapter, with countless victories; these include his heroic performance during the scouring of Truan IX, the crushing of the new Techno-Revivalist uprising on Faze V and his bold manoeuvres and personal fighting prowess during the Vendetta Campaign.

When the old Supreme Grand Master dies, his choice of successor is named and ceremonially presented with the panoply of the rank. Accompanied by the Inner Circle, he descends into ever deeper levels of the Rock, the Keeper of the Keys unlocking each adamantium door until the domed Chamber of Passageways is reached. From out of the shadows glide the mysterious Watchers in the Dark, to present the Supreme Grand Master with the Lion Helm and the Sword of Secrets. With these powerful icons of the Chapter, the new Supreme Grand Master is led down long hallways by the Watchers in the Dark until, at last, they come to the Arch of Truth. Alone, the Supreme Grand Master must enter, and on rare occasions the aspirant does not return: an unspoken test determines his resolve and his suitability for the role, and only if he is approved by the Watchers in the Dark will he be presented as Supreme Grand Master to the gathered Dark Angels brethren above. Amidst many vows and hymnals, the honorific title of Keeper of the Truth is bestowed, and the new Supreme Grand Master dons the Lion Helm and receives the silent salute of his entire Chapter.

As Supreme Grand Master, Azrael has proven to be a dynamic leader – a beacon of inspiration for those that fight alongside him and a visage of terror to his foes. Although solemn by nature and not given to elaborate speeches or flowery language, when he does speak, his words carry the conviction of righteousness and the surety of victory.

RITUALS OF THE DARK ANGELS

The Dark Angels hold to many ancient rites and traditions, from the Feast of the Malediction to the three day Mindchant of the Iron Penance. Most sacraments are led by the Dark Angels Chaplains, often accompanied by Company Masters. Some are instructional, some involve oath-taking, while others are mysterious, leaving the neophytes in awe at the unusual proceedings. All, however, are dour ceremonies, for the Sons of the Lion are a serious-minded Chapter who believe in a singularity of purpose – that of absolute devotion towards battling the Imperium's foes. Though they seem prosaic, none of the Dark Angels' ceremonies are without purpose; whether or not the participants understand it is another matter. Through devotion to these traditions, the Masters strive to make their Dark Angels brethren stronger – in mind, body and spirit – for in the wars to be, only the most resolute will survive.

In battle, Azrael commands his Chapter flawlessly – able to quickly grasp the strategic situation and orchestrate his forces to maximum advantage. His ability to coordinate multiple taskforces as well as the most minute detail of individual squad movements is extraordinary even for a Space Marine. Yet never does Azrael lose sight of the Dark Angels' secret agenda – even in the midst of a life-or-death battle, the hunt for the Fallen always continues.

Following in the mighty footsteps of the father of the Dark Angels, Primarch Lion El'Jonson, Azrael has proven a master at planning and executing an assault. Yet the fortunes of war do not always allow for the formulation of interlocking tactical manoeuvres, and in such cases, Azrael has proven time and again that his martial skills are second to none. It was Azrael that held the thin green line of Dark Angels against the red tide that broke against it when the Warp anomaly on the planet of Amity turned into a full-fledged daemonic incursion. Azrael alone kept doom at bay with his keen eye for defensive ground, his ability to inspire loyalty in his brethren and, in the end, through combat so fierce that the Sword of Secrets continued to smoke with Daemon ichor for many days afterwards.

Heedless of the laurels heaped upon him and his Chapter, Azrael is obdurate and unmoved by such adornment, his keen mind already working towards the next battle, the next sector to be brought under surveillance. As Supreme Grand Master of the Dark Angels, Azrael understands full well the tremendous heritage and duty of his station – the commander of what remains of the Emperor's First Legion. He alone is privy to the darkest secrets of the Chapter, and it is his honour to lead the quest for redemption. No matter the losses, no matter the consequences, the war must go on.

	WS	BS	S	T	W	I	A	Ld	Sv
Azrael	6	5	4	4	4	5	4	10	2+

UNIT TYPE: Infantry (Character).

WARGEAR: Bolt pistol, frag grenades, krak grenades.

WARLORD TRAIT: If Azrael is in your army, he must be the Warlord. He can choose any one of the Dark Angels Warlord Traits on page 28 (there is no need to roll).

SPECIAL RULES: Independent Character, Inner Circle (pg 28).

Rites of Battle: If Azrael is on the battlefield, all models from this codex use his Leadership for Morale, Pinning or Leadership tests.

Chapter Relics

Lion Helm: *An ancient artefact, the Lion Helm is said to have been worn by Lion El'Jonson himself. As with all heirlooms connected to the mighty Primarch of the Dark Angels, it is attended by the Watchers in the Dark. The helm generates a powerful force field that has protected the Supreme Grand Master since the days when the Dark Angels were still a Legion. To don that winged helmet is to take up the mantle of the Lion and lead the Dark Angels to victory, or die in the attempt.*

The Lion Helm is carried by the mysterious Helmet Bearer, which is represented on the tabletop by a separate miniature that will always remain as close as possible to Azrael. The model itself plays no part in the game; if the model gets in the way, simply move it to one side. If Azrael is killed, the Helmet Bearer is also removed.

The Lion Helm confers a 4+ invulnerable save to Azrael and his unit.

Lion's Wrath: *This legendary gun was made by Technomagos Prestor the Unchallenged in the days following the Fall of Caliban. Upon his elevation, Azrael added his name to the list of Dark Angels heroes that have borne it into battle down the ages.*

The Lion's Wrath is a combi-weapon with the Master-crafted special rule, with a secondary plasma gun with the following profile:

Range	S	AP	Type
24"	7	2	Rapid Fire, Blind, Gets Hot, Master-crafted

Protector: *A finely wrought suit of power armour, the Protector is inlaid with the sombre symbols of the Dark Angels. Its exact age is unknown, but the Protector has been considered a Chapter relic since the early years of M37, when it is recorded in Chapter records that it saved Brother Methias, Master of the 5th Company, from a close range battle cannon shot during the storming of the traitor stronghold on the moons of Secclucious VII. Since those days, the suit of armour regularly turns up in the Master of the Armoury's log, where it is praised for its exceptional ability to shrug off the most lethal of blows.*

The Protector is a suit of artificer armour (pg 65). Additionally, the Protector gives Azrael the Feel No Pain (6+) special rule.

Sword of Secrets: *The Sword of Secrets is a power sword that was created soon after the disappearance of Lion El'Jonson. It is the mightiest of the so-called Heavenfall Blades, the swords cut from a block of jet-black obsidian that struck the Rock whilst in orbit around the feral planet of Al Baradad. The blade of the Sword of Secrets is so incredibly well-crafted that it has not chipped nor lost its razor-sharp edge over its many millennia of bloody use. Only the Supreme Grand Master knows that it is also the only device that allows access to the deepest known dungeon in the Rock. Fitting the blade into a cleft in the wall unlocks the iron gate leading to a dark tunnel and the rune-protected cell in which the arch-heretic Luther is imprisoned.*

Range	S	AP	Type
-	+2	3	Melee, Master-crafted

Ezekiel

GRAND MASTER OF LIBRARIANS, HOLDER OF THE KEYS, KEEPER OF THE BOOK OF SALVATION

Ezekiel, the Dark Angels' Grand Master of Librarians, has the power to kill with but a thought. He can read the minds of friend or foe, and even the bravest feel unsettled under his penetrating gaze. For some, this unease stems from Ezekiel's crude bionic eye, yet Space Marines are accustomed to horrific injuries. Rather, it is Ezekiel's mien – a single glance of his good eye reveals the look of one who has stared deeply into the soul of Man and has found something lacking.

It is the Grand Master of Librarians' duty to bear the Book of Salvation and to use his powers to probe minds, assisting the Interrogator-Chaplains in their grim role. It is also Ezekiel's task to offer final judgement on those considered for elevation into the Inner Circle. He reaches into the recesses of a candidate's mind, seeking to reveal any taint or weakness. To his credit, every Inner Circle member inducted during his stewardship has remained steadfast. Finally, as the Chapter's Holder of the Keys, it is Ezekiel's burden to carry the keys that unlock all the doors within the Rock, save one.

	WS	BS	S	T	W	I	A	Ld	Sv
Ezekiel	5	5	4	4	3	5	3	10	2+

UNIT TYPE: **Infantry (Character).**

WARGEAR: **Artificer armour** (pg 65), **master-crafted bolt pistol, frag grenades, krak grenades, psychic hood.**

WARLORD TRAIT: **The Hunt** (pg 28).

SPECIAL RULES: **Inner Circle** (pg 28), **Independent Character, Psyker (Mastery Level 3).**

PSYKER: Ezekiel always knows the *Mind Worm* psychic power. He may generate two more powers from the **Divination**, **Pyromancy**, **Telepathy** and **Telekinesis** disciplines.

MIND WORM .... WARP CHARGE 1

Ezekiel burrows his consciousness into a victim's brain, forcing him to reveal his innermost secrets as he convulses to death.

Mind Worm is a **focussed witchfire** power with the following profile:

Range	S	AP	Type
12"	4	2	Assault D3, Ignores Cover, Sap Will

Sap Will: For each unsaved Wound a model suffers from *Mind Worm*, that model's Weapon Skill, Ballistic Skill, Initiative and Leadership are reduced by 3 (to a minimum of 1) for the remainder of the game.

Chapter Relics

Book of Salvation: *This revered tome lists the names of all the Fallen who have been captured by the Dark Angels. Only the Inner Circle know the contents of the book, but the whole Chapter understands that its protection is paramount.*

So long as Ezekiel lives, all friendly Dark Angels units within 6" of him fight with righteous vigour, adding 1 to their Weapon Skill characteristic.

Traitor's Bane: *This sword was made to slay those who dared turn their back on the Emperor. The rage of those betrayed is bound within this blade and, from the shrieks emitted by the traitors slain by it, their end is painful indeed.*

Range	S	AP	Type
-	User	3	Melee, Force, Master-crafted, Two-handed

Asmodai

MASTER INTERROGATOR-CHAPLAIN, MASTER OF REPENTANCE

The most sinister of the Dark Angels is Brother Asmodai, the Chapter's oldest and most successful Interrogator-Chaplain. Brutal, uncompromising and to the point, Asmodai does not suffer fools, nor does he tolerate idleness of mind or spirit. In his obsession, which has grown with his age, Asmodai has become a living embodiment of duty, openly disdaining all that does not pertain to battle, the Chapter's goals, and ultimately, to the secret hunt that drives him. Whether on the battlefield, at council with the Inner Circle, or in the dungeons administering to one of the heretical Fallen – or anyone who might have information about them – Asmodai is a merciless bringer of death, a true Dark Angel.

Asmodai's relentless nature and single-minded pursuit of the Fallen balances on the border of what is defensible. While his determination to force those that fall into his clutches to speak their secrets has aided the Chapter's mission immeasurably, more than once the Supreme Grand Master has been forced to censure Asmodai's demands, counteract his orders or cover up some of the Master Interrogator-Chaplain's more flagrant excesses. No Dark Angel better exemplifies the phrase 'the end justifies the means' than Asmodai, for in his unquenchable obsession, he is willing to sacrifice anything to capture another of the Fallen, and there is no boundary he will not cross to add another black pearl to his collection.

It was Asmodai who ordered the slaughter of all new recruits from the planet Narcium because their lacklustre answers to his questions raised the fear of gene-stock contamination. It was Asmodai who, upon hearing the frivolity of laughter in the halls of the Rock, placed the Penance of Silence upon the 7th Company. For a standard Terran year, the formation was unable to utter a sound save for hymnals and in-battle communications. However, such ardent discipline has its uses. Like any Chaplain, Asmodai chants the Liturgies of Battle, preaching the purity of hate to help each Dark Angel to focus his rage and become a killing machine. In combat, Asmodai further amplifies his zeal, inciting the fighting spirits of his battle-brothers to a fever pitch. It was Asmodai who led the forlorn hope to break into the Traitor of Rhun's palace and who inspired the impressive stand when his forces were isolated on the Daemon world of Amity.

Across countless battlefields, his reputation alone has struck fear into the hearts of the most hardened foes. With his matchless determination and will of iron, Asmodai ensures the Deathwing's mission is always completed.

	WS	BS	S	T	W	I	A	Ld	Sv
Asmodai	5	5	4	4	3	5	3	10	3+

UNIT TYPE: **Infantry (Character).**

WARGEAR: **Power armour** (pg 65), **crozius arcanum** (pg 62), **frag grenades, krak grenades, rosarius** (pg 64).

WARLORD TRAIT: **The Hunt** (pg 28).

SPECIAL RULES: **Fear, Independent Character, Inner Circle** (pg 28), **Zealot.**

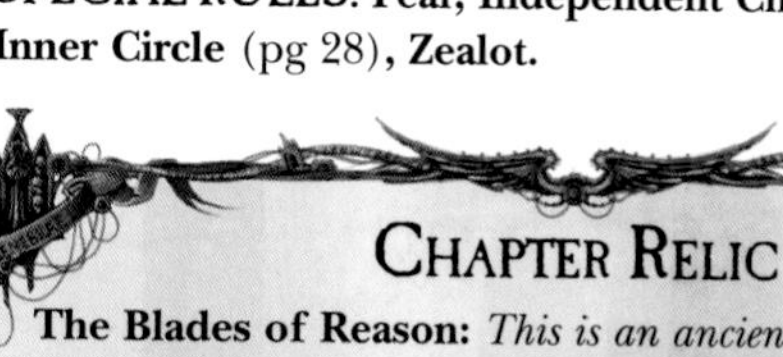

Chapter Relic

The Blades of Reason: *This is an ancient and horrific device, full of arcane cruelty and the sorrow of Mankind. Its many sharply honed and well-polished blades are etched with scriptures of repentance, and criss-crossing the weapon's head are cables and fine neural-wires, mystic science that amplifies pain to agonies beyond endurance.*

Range	S	AP	Type
-	User	-	Melee, Instant Death, Specialist Weapon

Belial

GRAND MASTER OF THE DEATHWING, BEARER OF THE SWORD OF SILENCE

To be named the Grand Master of the Deathwing is to be named a lion of the battlefield, a tactician without peer and the Chapter's most loyal paladin. Grand Master Belial, to whom the title currently belongs, has earned such an honour with deeds that would fill volumes, if the Dark Angels allowed such things to be written.

Belial is a warrior born – a killer whose skill with bolter and blade have always stood out, even amongst his superhuman brethren. His martial prowess is without style or artifice; there is no flourish to Belial's swordplay, no extravagance to his movements. Yet even as a neophyte, none but the Masters could best him in practice. Throughout his rise through the ranks, it was noted that Brother Belial was a perfectionist – chastising himself for a single missed shot. As a commander, Belial did not revel in triumphs, but instead, he begrudged the losses, castigating himself for the least mistake. Those beneath him came to expect that, after each action – even the most glorious victories – Belial would find them and assign each his own specific penitence, be it battle drills, hymnals, or arduous rites of atonement. Such discipline was not lamented, but embraced – for it was easy to see that Belial was righteous and his success undeniable.

While fighting against the Black Crusade of Furion, Belial slew the Chaos Lord of Khorne in single combat. For this deed, Supreme Grand Master Azrael promoted Belial to the rank of Master and presented him with a Chapter relic – the ancient Sword of Silence. In the Battle for Piscina IV, Belial distinguished himself yet further, fighting a delaying battle against superior odds. After Grand Master Gabriel's death aboard the Space Hulk *Charnel Shrine*, Belial was selected to command the Dark Angels 1st Company. Under his austere and exacting leadership, the Deathwing continues to earn praise in the fighting around the Eye of Terror, winning victories on the marshes of Crassia II and routing the Violators on the planet Terraq after a brutal campaign.

Amongst all the Dark Angels, there are none who judge themselves more abrasively than Belial. To the Grand Master of the 1st Company, every battle-brother lost, every foe not efficiently slain, only makes the defence of the Imperium of Man, and the path to Redemption, that much more difficult.

	WS	BS	S	T	W	I	A	Ld	Sv
Belial	6	5	4	4	3	5	3	10	2+

UNIT TYPE: **Infantry (Character).**

WARGEAR: **Terminator armour** (pg 65), **storm bolter, iron halo, teleport homer** (pg 64).

WARLORD TRAIT: **The Hunt** (pg 28).

SPECIAL RULES: **Deathwing Assault** (pg 44), **Independent Character, Inner Circle** (pg 28), **Vengeful Strike** (pg 44).

Marked for Retribution: Belial's shooting attacks are Precision Shots on a To Hit roll of 5+.

Tactical Precision: Belial (and any unit comosed entirely of models with the Inner Circle special rule that he has joined) do not scatter when arriving by Deep Strike.

Chapter Relic

Sword of Silence: *A power weapon crafted from the same meteorite as the Sword of Secrets, the Sword of Silence has traditionally been gifted to the most lethal close-quarters combatant in the Dark Angels. The Sword of Silence seems to swallow nearby light and sound, absorbing them into its glowing obsidian blade.*

Range	S	AP	Type
-	User	3	Melee, Fleshbane, Master-crafted

The Battle for Piscina IV

Piscina IV is a planet covered in teeming oceans and dotted with chains of volcanic islands. The Dark Angels utilise the world for recruitment, having built a great cathedral there in the 39th Millennium. At the time of the great Ork invasion of 221997.M41, however, only the Dark Angels 3rd Company, along with elements from the Deathwing and Ravenwing, were nearby. The Orks were led by Warlord Ghazghkull Mag Uruk Thraka, the most formidable greenskin in the galaxy. His assault caught the world by surprise, as no space hulks or roks had been detected entering the system. Instead, the Orks landed troops on the surface by way of long-ranged 'Telly-porta' technology that was masterminded by Nazdreg, an ostentatious Bad Moon Warboss nearly as powerful as Ghazghkull himself. Ghazghkull's first move was to teleport himself and a sizeable force from Scylla, *their distant space hulk. Before the full invasion force could be sent, however, the Orks ran out of power to fuel their still-experimental telly-porta. In order to bring reinforcements from their hulk, not to mention their full arsenal of enormous Gargants, Stompas and Battlewagon battalions, the Orks needed more energy. They quickly captured a power plant at their landing site and converted it to their nefarious purpose, but they needed more power and Ghazghkull led an assault to capture the power plant of Piscina IV's capital hive – Kadillus Harbour.*

The small contingent of Dark Angels stationed nearby responded, and soon the Orks and Space Marines were locked in deadly close quarters battles in the city around the power plant. A counter-attack by Company Master Belial (then the Master of the 3rd Company) sent the Orks reeling, but spurred on by Ghazghkull, they soon returned to press their advantage. The Dark Angels' basilica changed hands so many times its walls became soaked with blood. In a desperate move to halt the Orks, Belial confronted Ghazghkull. Though a mighty warrior, he was no match for the enormous Warlord and the Dark Angel was struck down, wounded almost unto death as the Orks assumed control of the second power plant.

With the telly-portas again operational, the battle for Piscina IV began in earnest, and more Orks appeared at the landing site. The wounded Belial, a consummate warrior, rallied to led the Dark Angels despite being outnumbered many thousands to one. In order to keep the Ork forces from uniting, Belial ordered a holding force to make a stand at the intervening Koth Ridge – a name that will forever resonate in the Chapter's history for the heroics performed there. Time and again, Ork assaults were hurled back at great loss. Knowing that his forces would eventually be overwhelmed, Master Belial led a daring Deathwing assault to destroy the Ork landing site, and partially succeeded in delaying the Ork reinforcements. Desperate for more power, Nazdreg himself countered with a surprise assault to seize a third power station at Barrak Gorge. If the Ork forces could combine their power sources, they would be able to teleport in their heavy battalions to truly dominate Piscina IV. Nazdreg launched an all-out assault, while Ghazghkull tried to move out of Kadillus Harbour. Through sheer tenacity alone, the Dark Angels held on until the remainder of their Chapter arrived to systematically recapture the power stations and destroy the Orks. Sensing failure, Ghazghkull returned to his distant space hulk, abandoning many Orks to the merciless Angels of Death. Thanks to the actions of Master Belial and his small force, Piscina IV was saved, and Ghazghkull's system-spanning ambitions held in check, at least until his attack upon the Armageddon system.

SAMMAEL

GRAND MASTER OF THE RAVENWING AND LEADER OF THE HUNT

It is a Master's place to lead his company in war, and throughout the battle-ridden history of the Dark Angels, no Company has suffered more leaders slain in duty than the Ravenwing. Given the number of dangerous battlefield roles the fabled 2nd Company performs, it is a testament of supreme skill that the Masters survive as long as they do. The present leader of the Ravenwing, Grand Master Sammael, is the 348th to lead the 2nd Company since the Dark Angels Legion was reformed into Chapters. Brother Sammael's promotion to his current office came more than a century ago as Gideon, the previous Master, lay dying, his body shattered by the Chaos Titan *Traitorous Ire*. Through blood-flecked lips, the old Master declared his successor, passing on the Raven Sword as he breathed his last.

Sammael is bold to the point of being reckless – a trait required in order to head a mobile company whose success depends upon speed and hard-hitting surprise. Despite his well-noted audacity, Sammael's reign at the head of the Company has already been unusually long and successful. Although masterful at orchestrating distracting manoeuvres and feints, if given a chance, Sammael much prefers to take matters into his own hands. From the saddle of *Corvex*, his jetbike, a relic from the bygone Age of Technology, Grand Master Sammael cuts down any foolish enough to face him. In battle he wields the razor-honed Raven Sword, an heirloom that has served all Ravenwing Masters before him.

It was on his jetbike that Sammael dodged between battlesuits to cut the Ethereal Sha Aux'Phan in twain, securing victory in the Auxion campaign. It was Sammael's personal heroics in an epic duel that allowed him to run the pretender Kaligar to ground during the Fourth Quadrant Rebellion. Though it was never revealed, Kaligar was a long-sought member of the Fallen, and his capture was greatly lauded by the Inner Circle. The aerial stunts Sammael performed while leading the 2nd Company in the war against the Orks of Charadon are legendary, even amongst the greenskins, a xenos race much noted for their high speed and brazen vehicle manoeuvres.

CORVEX

During the Horus Heresy, many Space Marine Legions could field formations mounted upon jetbikes, but Mankind has lost the secrets of building these anti-gravitic craft. The last of the Imperium's venerable Mark XIVs disappeared centuries ago. The Grand Master of the Ravenwing, however, still rides into battle upon a jetbike, a prized vehicle known as Corvex. *It bears front-mounted storm bolters and an underslung plasma cannon – its fusion generator capable of powering hundreds of shots. Many times* Corvex *has been thought lost or destroyed, but always returns. Whether the Dark Angels maintain a cache of relics or have long-lost STC material is unknown, as they do not share their secrets.*

What makes Grand Master Sammael such a masterful commander of the Ravenwing is that he knows when to temper his penchant for close combat and when to call in aid. To the Ravenwing alone is entrusted the task of setting the homers that allow the Deathwing Terminators to teleport accurately onto the battlefield. Of the whole company, none are more daring about planting the beacons in the very midst of the foe than Grand Master Sammael. Though he prefers to set about this hazardous task from the back of his jetbike, he sometimes takes to the field in his modified Land Speeder, *Sableclaw.* This powerful vehicle is protected by the Shield of Night, a force field of ancient artifice which protects the Grand Master from enemy fire.

Although the Ravenwing are known across the galaxy as the most elite mobile strike force in the Imperium, none but Grand Master Sammael and his trusted Black Knights know the full details of their company's true purpose. Sammael's task is to seek out and capture the Fallen, all the while ensuring that the majority of his black-clad hunters never learn too much about the nature of their quarry.

	WS	BS	S	T	W	I	A	Ld	Sv
Sammael	6	5	4	5	3	5	3	10	3+

UNIT TYPE: **Jetbike (Character).**

WARGEAR: **Power armour** (pg 65), **bolt pistol, frag grenades, krak grenades, teleport homer** (pg 64).

WARLORD TRAIT: **Rapid Manoeuvre** (pg 28).

SPECIAL RULES: **Hit & Run, Independent Character, Inner Circle** (pg 28), **Scouts, Skilled Rider.**

UPGRADE:

Sableclaw: Should you choose to field Sammael mounted on his Land Speeder instead of on his jetbike, the following profile is used instead.

		Armour			
	BS	F	S	R	HP
Sableclaw	5	14	14	10	2

UNIT TYPE: **Vehicle (Fast, Skimmer).**

WARGEAR: **Twin-linked assault cannon and twin-linked heavy bolter.**

SPECIAL RULES: **Deep Strike.**

Chapter Relics

Adamantine Mantle: *Blessed in a special ritual by the Interrogator-Chaplains within their Inner Sanctum far beneath the Tower of Angels, this cloak is interwoven with rare minerals and fibres from the fabled Cloak of the Lion.*

The Adamantine Mantle grants Sammael the Eternal Warrior special rule.

Corvex: *A treasured wonder from a distant age,* Corvex *is as sleek as it is powerful. It is held aloft by gravitic drives, the likes of which are lost to the Techpriests. To see* Corvex *streak across the battlefield is to know that the Ravenwing are on the hunt!*

Corvex is a jetbike fitted with a plasma cannon and a twin-linked storm bolter.

Night Halo: *This Dark Angels icon is a symbol of bravery and a ward against the weapons of the enemy. It has served many Masters of the Ravenwing and Sammael's faith in its protective powers has proved well founded over his many years of battle.*

The Night Halo grants Sammael a 4+ invulnerable save. If Sammael is riding in *Sableclaw,* it instead grants the Land Speeder a 4+ invulnerable save.

Raven Sword: *This sword is one of a trio of blades fabricated out of a meteorite that struck the Rock at Al Baradad, shortly after the fall of Caliban. It was named the Raven Sword, for it is traditionally the weapon of the Grand Master of the Ravenwing. Like the two other relics whose origin it shares, the Raven Sword has a razor-sharp edge that has never dulled. Alone amongst its brothers, however, it makes a low keening sound when swung that few foes have heard and lived to tell of.*

Range	S	AP	Type
-	User	2	Melee, Master-crafted

ARMOURY OF THE ROCK

This section of *Codex: Dark Angels* lists the weapons and equipment used by the Dark Angels and their Successor Chapters, along with the rules for using them in your games of Warhammer 40,000. Equipment that is carried by named special characters is detailed in the appropriate entry in the Unforgiven section (pages 52 to 59), while weapons and equipment used by all the other types of units are detailed here.

RANGED WEAPONS

Rules for the following ranged weapons can be found in the *Warhammer 40,000* rulebook:

- Assault cannon
- Autocannon
- Boltgun
- Bolt pistol
- Combi-weapons
- Flamer
- Flamestorm cannon
- Heavy bolter
- Heavy flamer
- Lascannon
- Melta bomb
- Meltagun
- Missile launcher
- Multi-melta
- Plasma cannon
- Plasma gun
- Plasma pistol
- Sniper rifle
- Space Marine shotgun
- Storm bolter

AVENGER MEGA BOLTER

A smaller version of the Vulcan mega bolter, the avenger pattern mega bolter is a formidable rapid-firing weapon. Nose-mounted on the Nephilim Jetfighters, they have proven ideal for engaging opposition flyers in deadly dogfights, and can carve through enemy infantry and vehicle squadrons on strafing runs.

Range	S	AP	Type
48"	6	4	Heavy 5

BLACKSWORD MISSILES

Designed to fit under the wings of the Nephilim Jetfighters, these missiles take their name from the ominous black contrails they leave in their wake, and are used primarily to bring down enemy flyers and light ground vehicles.

Range	S	AP	Type
36"	6	4	Heavy 1, One use only

CYCLONE MISSILE LAUNCHER

The cyclone is an efficient missile launcher system used by Space Marines in Terminator armour to provide heavy fire support. Fitted onto the carapace of a Terminator, the cyclone missile launcher enables its bearer to engage both heavily armoured vehicles with super-charged krak missiles, and massed, lightly armoured infantry with its frag missiles.

A Terminator can fire his cyclone missile launcher in addition to his storm bolter.

	Range	S	AP	Type
Frag Missile	48"	4	6	Heavy 2, Blast
Krak missile	48"	8	3	Heavy 2

DEATHWIND LAUNCHER

The short-ranged but powerful deathwind launcher lays down an intense carpet of explosions, ideal for clearing a beachhead for Drop Pods that land in the midst of enemy troops.

Some Drop Pods are upgraded to carry a deathwind launcher in place of a storm bolter.

Range	S	AP	Type
12"	5	-	Heavy 1, Large Blast

DEMOLISHER CANNON

The demolisher cannon is the weapon of choice when faced with dug-in enemy infantry in a dense environment. A single one of its terrific blasts is even capable of bringing down entire buildings.

Range	S	AP	Type
24"	10	2	Ordnance 1, Large Blast

HURRICANE BOLTER

There are few anti-infantry weapons that can mow down the enemy like the hurricane bolter, wiping out entire squads at a time.

A hurricane bolter consists of three twin-linked boltguns fired as a single weapon.

PLASMA STORM BATTERY

The plasma storm battery is an ancient weapon that can fire in two modes – a rapid burst mode, or a slower, supercharged mode that sends a toroid of plasma to explode over a larger area.

	Range	S	AP	Type
Burst mode	24"	7	2	Heavy 3, Gets Hot
Charged mode	24"	7	2	Heavy 1, Gets Hot, Large Blast

PLASMA TALON

Raven-pattern bikes have their twin-linked boltguns replaced with a weapon unique to the Unforgiven Chapters, the plasma talon. With a range in between the plasma pistol and plasma gun, the plasma talon gives the Black Knights a significant boost in firepower.

Range	S	AP	Type
18"	7	2	Gets Hot, Twin-linked

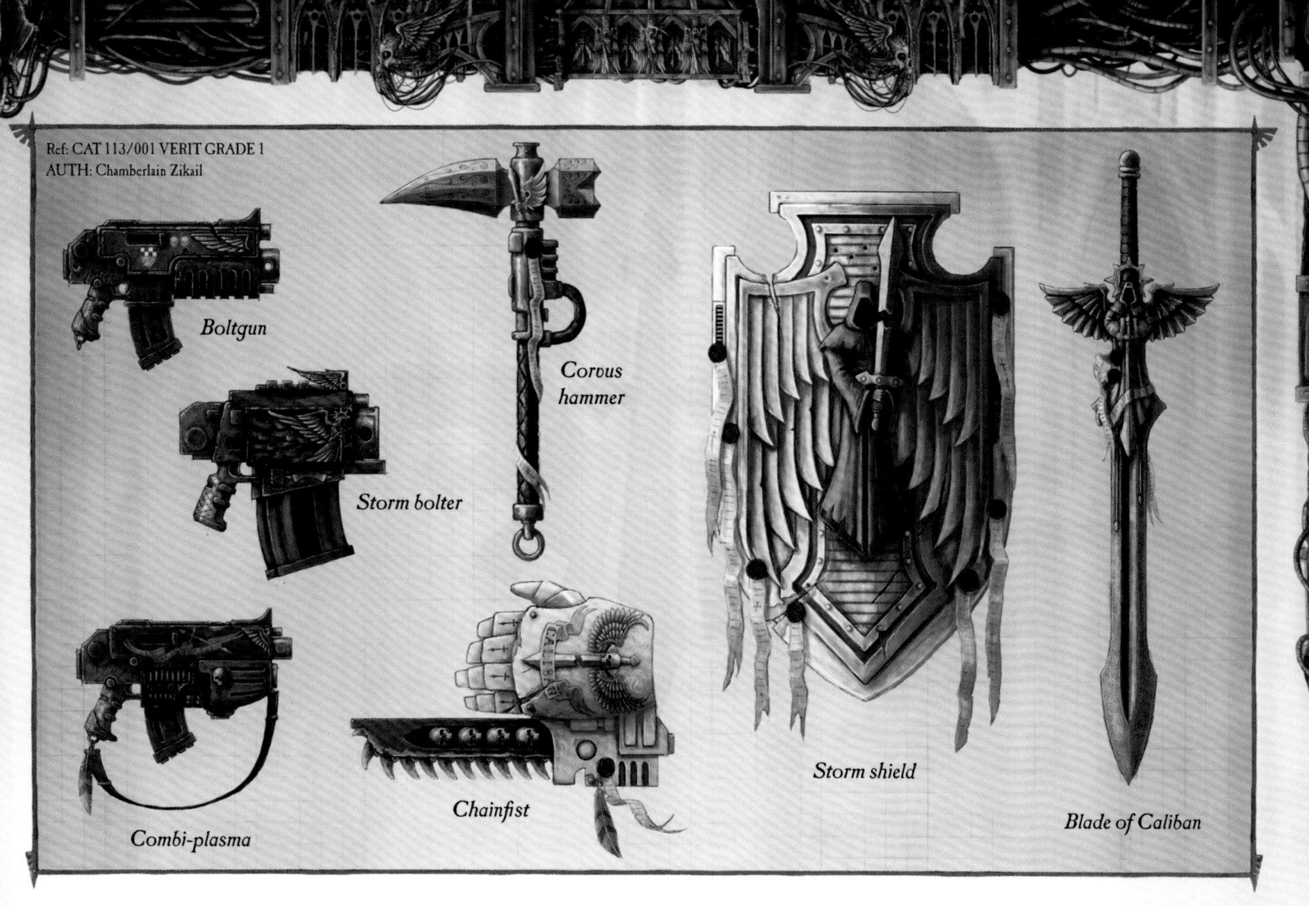

Ravenwing Grenade Launcher

Ravenwing Black Knights employ grenade launchers adapted to fire even at the high speeds at which they race across the battlefield. These grenade launchers fire specialised shells utilising ancient technologies. The rad shell spreads contaminated fragments that have a debilitating effect on a foe, while the stasis shell momentarily freezes time, slowing the reactions of any nearby.

	Range	S	AP	Type
Frag shell	24"	3	6	Rapid Fire, Blast
Krak shell	24"	6	4	Rapid Fire,
Rad shell	12"	3	-	Assault 1, Blast, Rad Charge
Stasis shell	12"	-	-	Assault 1, Blast, Stasis Anomaly

Rad Charge: Every model in a unit hit by one or more rad shells suffers a -1 penalty to their Toughness until the end of the turn (this can affect the victims' Instant Death threshold).

Stasis Anomaly. Every model in a unit hit by one or more weapons with this special rule suffers a -1 penalty to their Weapon Skill and Initiative until the end of the turn.

Rift Cannon

The scintillating beam of the rift cannon cracks a hole in reality itself, creating a deadly implosion. Those who survive the blast suffer the stunning effect of even so brief an exposure to such an unusual phenomenon.

Range	S	AP	Type
18"	5	-	Heavy 1, Blast, Blind

Stasis Bomb

The stasis bomb combines explosives with ancient and little understood technology that halts the normal flow of time, causing any not slain by the blast to feel momentarily disorientated.

Range	S	AP	Type
-	3	-	Heavy 1, Bomb, Large Blast, Vast Stasis Anomaly, One use only

Vast Stasis Anomaly: Any unit hit by one or more weapons with this special rule suffers a -3 penalty to its Weapon Skill and Initiative until the end of the turn. This replaces any penalty inflicted on the target by a Stasis Anomaly (see left).

Typhoon Missile Launcher

This versatile weapon is specially adapted for high-speed assaults.

	Range	S	AP	Type
Frag missiles	48"	4	6	Heavy 2, Blast
Krak missiles	48"	8	3	Heavy 2

Whirlwind Multiple Missile Launcher

Whirlwinds utilise vengeance missiles to engage enemy infantry, and incendiary castellan missiles, to blast foes entrenched within cover.

	Range	S	AP	Type
Vengeance missiles	12-48"	5	4	Ordnance 1, Barrage, Large Blast
Incendiary castellan missiles	12-48"	4	5	Ordnance 1, Barrage, Ignores Cover, Large Blast

Melee Weapons

Rules for the following Melee weapons can be found in the *Warhammer 40,000* rulebook:

- Chainfist
- Chainsword
- Close combat weapon
- Force weapons
- Lightning claws
- Power fist
- Power weapons
- Thunder hammer

Blade of Caliban

Blades of Caliban are relics and each has its own honourable heritage. Only the Champions of each company, having performed heroic and faultless duty, earn the right to wield one of these blades.

Range	S	AP	Type
-	+1	3	Melee, Unwieldy

Corvus Hammer

On Caliban the thick forests made tall lances impractical, so the knights developed a unique military pick, which consisted of a hammerhead modified to provide additional power during impact. Its beak-like spike proved ideal for puncturing monster scales and armour alike. The bike-mounted warriors of the Dark Angels Legion adopted this weapon design and these ancient weapons are still maintained by the Black Knights.

Range	S	AP	Type
-	+1	-	Melee, Rending

Crozius Arcanum

The crozius serves as both a sacred staff of office and a weapon for Dark Angels Chaplains and Interrogator-Chaplains. An energy field boosts the crozius arcanum's mauling power.

Range	S	AP	Type
-	+2	4	Melee, Concussive

Servo-arm

Techmarines and Servitors are equipped with powerful servo-arms that can be used for battlefield repairs or even put to use as weapons. These robotic arms are strong enough to lift heavy machine components, or to crush the life from a foe.

Range	S	AP	Type
-	x2	1	Melee, Unwieldy, Specialist Weapon

DEATHWING WEAPONS

The weapons carried by the Deathwing Knights and the Company Champion of the Deathwing all have the following special rule:

Bane of the Traitor: When a weapon with this special rule is used to attack a unit from *Codex: Chaos Space Marines,* the weapon's AP is improved by 1 (to a maximum of 1).

Mace of Absolution

Bespiked, glowing with power and emanating an eerie mist from their vents, these ominous weapons are employed by the Deathwing Knights in their endless hunt for the Fallen. In the presence of the most accursed heretics, their power is amplified to awe-inspiring magnitude.

	Range	S	AP	Type
normal	-	+2	4	Melee, Bane of the Traitor, Concussive
Smite mode	-	+6	2	Melee, Bane of the Traitor, Concussive, One use only*

** All models in the unit must use their Mace of Absolution's smite setting at the same time.*

Flail of the Unforgiven

The leaders of the Deathwing Knights eschew the maces of their fellows in favour of brutal flails. These archaic weapons are carried as a badge of office, and are a reminder to all the Fallen of their ultimate fate at the hands of the Dark Angels.

Range	S	AP	Type
-	+2	3	Melee, Bane of the Traitor, Concussive

Halberd of Caliban

The Company Champion of the Deathwing traditionally carries this massive weapon, reforged from a Blade of Caliban shattered in battle long ago, and incorporating the same grim technologies that power the weapons of the Deathwing Knights.

Range	S	AP	Type
-	+2	2	Melee, Bane of the Traitor, Two-handed

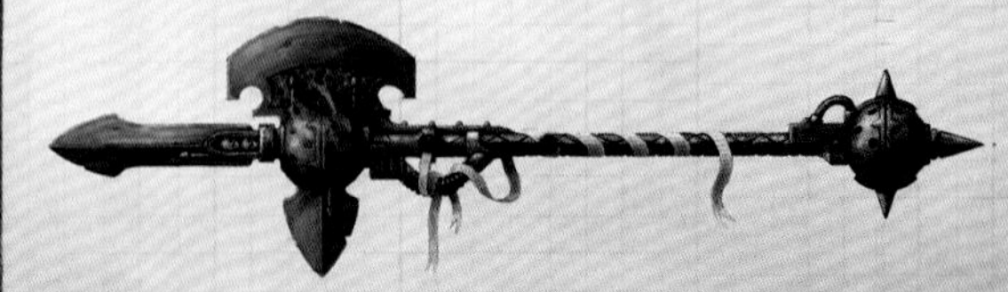

Special Issue Wargear

Rules for the following items are listed on the summary page (pg 105). The full rules can be found in the *Warhammer 40,000* rulebook.

Frag grenades* | Melta bombs
Krak grenades | Psychic hood

** See assault grenades*

Auspex

A short-ranged scanning device, the auspex uses a range of detection modes to pinpoint the location of hidden enemies. Using an auspex to triangulate a target, a Space Marine is better able to direct fire towards a foe secreted in even the densest cover.

A model with an auspex can use it in place of making a shooting attack. If he does so, target an enemy unit within 12" (this does not count as choosing a target for his unit to shoot at). A unit that is targeted by one or more auspexes has its cover saves reduced by 1 until the end of the phase.

Camo Cloak

Space Marine Scouts often wear camo cloaks – loose garments woven from light-absorbing material that imitates surrounding terrain. So garbed, Scouts blend perfectly into any landscape, making them hard to see at range and difficult targets when in cover of any kind.

A model wearing a camo cloak has +1 cover save. If they do not already have a cover save, they gain a 6+ cover save.

Combat Shield

A combat shield is a lighter version of a storm shield that is fitted to the arm of the wearer. This leaves the user's hand free to wield a pistol or other weapon, substituting a measure of defence for increased versatility.

A combat shield confers a 6+ invulnerable save.

Conversion Field

A conversion field creates an energy zone that surrounds and protects its user. The field will convert the force of incoming enemy shots or attacks into a brilliant flash of light that is more than capable of blinding nearby assailants.

A conversion field confers a 4+ invulnerable save. At the end of a phase in which the bearer passes one or more invulnerable saves granted by the conversion field, all units within D6" of the bearer must test as if they had been hit by a weapon with the Blind special rule. Friendly units can re-roll this test.

Digital Weapons

Digital weapons are concealed lasers fitted into finger rings, bionic implants or the knuckles of a power-armoured gauntlet. They lack the power to be used at long range, but can be triggered in close combat to take advantage of an exposed weakness while the enemy fends off the main attack.

A model armed with digital weapons can re-roll a single failed roll To Wound in each Assault phase.

Displacer Field

The displacer field is a strange, if somewhat risky device employed to protect an individual. The ancient and inexplicable technology will teleport its bearer out of harm's way should the field be struck by a powerful enough blow or shot. The displacer field activates automatically and the user cannot control the direction in which he will re-appear; he will simply blink back into a nearby position, which can sometimes result in an even more hazardous situation.

A model with a displacer field has a 3+ invulnerable save. At the end of a phase in which the bearer passes one or more saves granted by the displacer field, he suffers 'displacement'. When a model suffers displacement, it immediately scatters D6". If the scatter causes the bearer to arrive on top, or within 1", of another unit or impassable terrain, alter the scatter by the minimum amount possible (in any direction) to prevent this.

In the Assault phase, displacement instead happens at the end of the Initiative 1 step, after all blows have been struck, but before the assault result is calculated. If the displacement occurred when the bearer was locked in combat, he must make a Pile In move immediately after the displacement is resolved.

Infravisor

This simple visor allows a Space Marine to access a wide range of spectrums. So equipped, he can see better in low-light conditions than a normal human could see in optimal daylight.

A model with an infravisor has the Night Vision special rule. However, a unit that contains one or more models with an infravisor counts as Initiative 1 when taking Blind tests.

Iron Halo

The iron halo is a symbol of exceptional bravery and wisdom. It contains a powerful energy field that acts as a ward against the weapons of the enemy. An iron halo is capable of rendering useless even the most potent of attacks.

A model with an iron halo has a 4+ invulnerable save.

Jump Pack

A jump pack enables the wearer to make great bounding leaps across the battlefield and make a boosted flight over short distances. Space Marines often make use of airdrop deployment – troops wearing jump packs leaping from low-flying Thunderhawk Gunships and using controlled bursts to slow their descent to the battlefield.

Models equipped with jump packs gain the Jump unit type as described in the *Warhammer 40,000* rulebook.

Narthecium

This device, along with the reductor, is employed both to heal wounded Dark Angels and, if this is impossible, to remove their progenoid glands. These glands are the biological repositories of Space Marine gene-seed, and the future of the Chapter.

As long as the Apothecary is alive, all models in his unit have the Feel No Pain special rule.

PERFIDIOUS RELIC OF THE UNFORGIVEN

Ancient relics from the old Legion that have been recaptured by the Deathwing are sometimes carried into battle by the wraith-like figures known as Watchers in the Dark. The exact nature or function of most of these revered relics is unknown – they are as mysterious as the cowled figures that bear them. What is known is their effect on the battlefield – their presence alone dampens the power of enemy psykers and fills the Dark Angels' opponents with feelings of dread.

Perfidious Relics are borne to battle by the mysterious Watchers in the Dark. These beings are represented by their own separate miniature that will always remain as close as possible to the HQ choice or unit that selected them. The model itself plays no part in the game; if the model gets in the way, simply move it to one side. If the HQ choice or unit that selected the Perfidious Relic of the Unforgiven is slain, the Watcher in the Dark model is removed as well.

Models in a unit that includes a Perfidious Relic of the Unforgiven have the Adamantium Will and Fear special rules.

PORTA-RACK

This vile invention was devised in some long-forgotten dark age of Mankind and enhances its wicked potential through energy fields, neuro-stimulators, pain amplifiers and other spike-ridden accoutrements. When fully extended, the porta-rack is a foreboding torture-frame taller than a man. By activating its runes, however, the menacing device folds down upon itself until it finally collapses into a hand-sized object, easy to carry or store.

If the bearer kills an enemy character in close combat, then he gains the Fear and Preferred Enemy special rules. In addition, your army may now use any enemy teleport homers and locator beacons as if they were your own.

POWER FIELD GENERATOR

This potent artefact creates an energy field – a force bubble – that protects not only its wearer, but also all those within close proximity. Such devices offer a potent defence, but are not without complications. The power field generator cannot distinguish between friend and foe, and will shield any within its range.

A model with a power field generator, and all models (friendly and enemy) within 3" of a model with a power field generator, have a 4+ invulnerable save.

ROSARIUS

A rosarius is a gorget or amulet worn by Dark Angels Chaplains and Interrogator-Chaplains, both for protection and as a symbol of office. A rosarius emits a protective energy field around the wearer, and is capable of deflecting blows and shots that would smash a ferrocrete bunker. It is believed that the stronger its bearer's belief in the might of the Emperor, the stronger a rosarius' force field will be.

A model with a rosarius has a 4+ invulnerable save.

SERVO-HARNESS

A Techmarine can upgrade his servo-arm to a full servo-harness. This backpack-mounted contraption is a mobile shrine to the Omnissiah. It incorporates a great deal of tools, mechanical limbs and weapons, all of which better enable a Techmarine in the field to make battlefield repairs to vehicles, bolster defences, or to assist his brethren in combat.

A servo-harness gives the Techmarine an extra servo-arm, a plasma cutter and a flamer. In the Shooting phase, the Techmarine can fire both harness-mounted weapons, or one harness-mounted weapon and another weapon.

	Range	S	AP	Type
Plasma cutter	12"	7	2	Assault 1, Gets Hot, Twin-linked

SIGNUM

The signum is a special form of communication device that quickly processes and broadcasts targeting data. This ancient device allows one member of a Space Marine squad to fire with even greater accuracy, battering vital targets with a hail of unerring shots.

At the start of the Shooting phase, a model with a signum can choose to use it instead of shooting. If he does so, one model in his squad is Ballistic Skill 5 for the remainder of the Shooting phase. Declare that the signum is being used before any rolls To Hit are made.

SPACE MARINE BIKE

Space Marine bikes are fitted with powerful engines and bulletproof tyres. Each bike is a versatile fighting platform capable of moving at great speed while remaining steady enough that the rider can fire its armament. When used by a Space Marine to charge into combat, the speed and weight of the bike itself becomes a formidable weapon.

Models equipped with Space Marine bikes change their unit type to Bike as described in the *Warhammer 40,000* rulebook. Space Marine bikes are fitted with a twin-linked boltgun.

STORM SHIELD

A storm shield is a solid shield that has an energy field generator built into it. Though the bulk of the shield offers physical protection, much more impressive is the energy field, capable of deflecting almost any attack; blows that would normally cut through even Terminator armour are turned aside with ease.

A model with a storm shield has a 3+ invulnerable save. In addition, a model equipped with a storm shield can never claim the +1 bonus Attack for being armed with two Melee weapons in an assault.

TELEPORT HOMER

Teleport homers emit a powerful signal enabling orbiting Strike Cruisers to lock on to them with their teleportation equipment. By matching the exact coordinates of this signal, the risk of missing the intended mark is greatly reduced.

Friendly units composed entirely of models in Terminator armour do not scatter when they Deep Strike, so long as the first model is placed with 6" of the teleport homer's bearer. For this to work, the bearer of the teleport homer must have been on the board at the start of the turn.

Armour

Artificer Armour
Embellished by the finest artificers in the Dark Angels armoury, these lavish suits afford the wearer protection to rival even Terminators.

Artificer armour confers a 2+ Armour Save.

Power Armour
Made from thick ceramite plates and electrically motivated fibre bundles that enhance the movements of the wearer, power armour is the standard protection for Space Marines.

Power armour confers a 3+ Armour Save.

Scout Armour
Less cumbersome than power armour, scout armour is ideal for infiltration work and allows a greater freedom of motion.

Scout armour confers a 4+ Armour Save.

Terminator Armour
Terminator armour is the best protection a Space Marine can be equipped with. It is even said that Terminator armour can withstand the titanic energies at a plasma generator's core, and that this was, in fact, the armour's original purpose.

Terminator armour confers a 2+ Armour Save and a 5+ invulnerable save. Furthermore, models in Terminator armour have the Bulky, Deep Strike and Relentless special rules, and may not make Sweeping Advances.

Deathwing: Dark Angels characters equipped with Terminator armour gain the Deathwing Assault and Vengeful Strike special rules (pg 44).

Dark Angels Vehicle Equipment

Rules for the following vehicle upgrades can be found in the *Warhammer 40,000* rulebook:

Dozer blade
Extra armour
Hunter-killer missile
Searchlight
Smoke launchers
Storm bolter

Frag Assault Launchers
The hulls of Land Raider Crusaders and Land Raider Redeemers are studded with explosive charges designed to hurl shrapnel at the enemy as the troops inside charge out.

Any unit charging into close combat on the same turn as it disembarks from a Land Raider Crusader or Redeemer counts as having frag grenades.

Locator beacon
The locator beacon is a signalling package that contains a teleport homing device, broad-spectrum communicators and geo-positional tracking. When activated, the locator beacon streams detailed positional uploads in Adeptus Astartes coded signals, allowing for precision reinforcement by reserve forces.

Friendly units do not scatter when they Deep Strike, so long as the first model is placed with 6" of a model equipped with a locator beacon. The locator beacon must have been on the battlefield at the start of the turn in order for it to be used.

Siege Shield
Due to their frequent deployment in rubble-strewn cityfights or hive-assaults, many Vindicators are fitted with enormous siege shields. These dozer or assault blades allow the Vindicator to bulldoze through obstacles with ease.

A vehicle with a siege shield automatically passes Dangerous Terrain tests.

'The sins of heresy and treachery can never be repented.'

BANNERS & STANDARDS

As remnants of the First Legion, the Dark Angels carry to battle ancient banners, redolent with meaning and awe-inspiring in their effect upon the brethren of the Chapter.

When determining assault results, add 1 to your total if there are one or more friendly units with a banner or standard locked in that combat. Banners also have additional effects depending on their type, described here.

DARK ANGELS CHAPTER BANNER

Perhaps the greatest position of honour afforded any Dark Angel is to carry aloft the Chapter Banner into battle. In the presence of the Supreme Grand Master, and inspired by this glorious relic, the Dark Angels will surely prevail.

Friendly units from *Codex: Dark Angels* within 12" of the Chapter Banner re-roll failed Morale checks and Pinning tests. In addition, all friendly Dark Angels models in the same unit as this banner have +1 Attack whilst the bearer is alive.

COMPANY STANDARD

These banners are the embodiment of a company's fighting spirit on the battlefield, emblazoned with honour markings and the names of glorious campaigns. Every member of a company fights all the harder in their august presence.

Friendly units from *Codex: Dark Angels* within 12" of a Company Standard re-roll failed Morale checks and Pinning tests.

REVERED STANDARD

Many standards are oft-repaired or replaced, but some are so resonant with honours that they are instead protected by stasis in the Great Hall on the Rock, next to the Chapter's sacred standards. When they are taken to war, the entire Chapter rallies around them.

Friendly units from *Codex: Dark Angels* within 12" of a Revered Standard re-roll failed Morale checks and Pinning tests. In addition, all friendly units from *Codex: Dark Angels* within 6" of the model bearing the Revered Standard have the Crusader special rule.

RAVENWING COMPANY BANNER

In the Great Hall can be found the eldest of the Ravenwing banners, a venerable symbol to remind all of the power of reckless speed and undaunted courage. All who see it feel dread.

Any friendly Ravenwing unit within 12" of this banner automatically passes its Initiative test when attempting to Hit & Run, and rolls an additional dice when determining the distance of the Hit & Run move.

DEATHWING COMPANY BANNER

The Deathwing Company Banner is as legendary as the bone-white Terminator armour of the 1st Company. It has flown over countless victories and inspires the Deathwing to new heights of vengeance.

All friendly models with the Inner Circle special rule within 6" of the model bearing this banner gain +1 Attack.

SACRED STANDARDS

These three Dark Angels standards date back to the time of the Great Crusade. It is the custom for only one to be used at any time; the remaining two are held in the Great Hall on the rock.

Only one of the Sacred Standards may be chosen per army, even if you have more than one Command Squad (of any type) in your force.

STANDARD OF RETRIBUTION

The Standard of Retribution serves to remind the Dark Angels that the enemies of the Emperor can never be forgiven. In the shadow of this hallowed artefact, they are inspired to fight on under any circumstances, smiting their foes with righteous fury.

Any friendly *Codex: Dark Angels* unit within 12" of the model bearing this banner re-rolls failed Morale and Pinning tests. In addition, these units gain the Counter-attack special rule.

STANDARD OF FORTITUDE

This forbidding standard represents the unstoppable courage and tenacity for which the Chapter is famed. It will inspire any nearby Dark Angels to press the attack, heedless of incoming blows and bullets, advancing steadily while unleashing a hail of fire at the enemy.

Any friendly *Codex: Dark Angels* unit within 12" of the banner re-rolls failed Morale and Pinning tests. In addition, these units gain the Feel No Pain special rule.

STANDARD OF DEVASTATION

The Standard of Devastation is a symbol of defiance and devastating retaliation. Throughout its proud history, the banner has flown above numerous last stands and as legends have it, has been found many times atop heaped piles of the enemy dead.

Any friendly *Codex: Dark Angels* unit within 12" of this standard re-rolls failed Morale and Pinning tests. In addition, all friendly *Codex: Dark Angels* units within 6" of the standard treat their boltguns as Salvo 2/4 weapons.

Dark Angels Chapter Relics

These artefacts are items of incredible rarity, ancient heirlooms that are maintained in places of honour on the Rock. Only the mightiest of Dark Angels are worthy to use such storied items, and their heroics and deeds simply add to the continuing legends and myths of the items themselves. Only one of each of the following relics may be chosen per army – there is but one of each of these items in the galaxy!

Foe-Smiter

This ornate storm bolter was wrought by Fedorovich the Great, amongst the foremost weaponsmiths of the red planet during the age when the Tech-Priests joined with the Emperor's forces to equip the armies for the Great Crusade. It was he who forged so many of the master-crafted weapons still prized by the Imperium today, but even then, the weapon known as Foe-smiter was considered special. It was presented with honour to the first Legion of the Space Marines, where it was used to great effect by Brother Bartholomew – the first Grand Master of the Deathwing. To this day, Foe-smiter can still lay down a cavalcade of fire, and is highly prized by the Dark Angels.

Range	S	AP	Type
24"	4	4	Assault 3, Master-crafted

Lion's Roar

One of the most unusual pieces in the arsenal of the Rock is the combi-weapon known as the Lion's Roar. It is similar to the combi-weapon borne by Supreme Grand Master Azrael, although the single-shot plasma blast it fires is accompanied by a devastating roar (from whence the weapon gets its name). The Lion's Roar is issued to heroes of the Chapter and over the years it has proven to be the ideal weapon of choice for those leading boarding missions, bunker assaults, or a forlorn hope. Whether its heroic bearer returns from battle or not, the Lion's Wrath has always been recovered and returned to its place of honour in the Rock's armouries.

The Lion's Roar is a Master-crafted combi-weapon. The secondary weapon has the following profile:

Range	S	AP	Type
24"	7	2	Assault 1, Blast, Gets Hot, Master-crafted

Mace of Redemption

The Mace of Redemption is perhaps the greatest of the weapons forged by the Dark Angels to hunt their traitorous comrades. Blessed with incantations of vengeance, the hollow centre of this sacred power maul flares white hot when it smites a foe. It is said that, with this mace in hand, Supreme Grand Master Raphael struck down the Daemon Prince ruler of the blasphemous world of New Caliban, allowing the arch-heretic to be captured. Of all the Dark Angels who have ever hunted the Fallen, none has bested this heroic deed.

Range	S	AP	Type
-	+3	3	Melee, Bane of the Traitor*, Blind, Concussive

* *See Deathwing weapons, page 62.*

Monster Slayer of Caliban

This ancient weapon was traditionally bestowed upon the most honourable knight of the Order before the onset of a long quest into the wilds of Caliban. Its well-honed blade is empowered by a force generator of magnificent strength; however, over the ages, it has grown somewhat temperamental, and the know-how to fix such ancient technology has passed beyond what the Techmarines of the Dark Angels can repair. It is believed that as long as its owner stays pure of mind, the Monster Slayer of Caliban will strike down even the greatest of foes. This has been proven countless times, perhaps most famously when Master Mortifer wielded the blade to dispatch three hulking Carnifexes. It is said that Mortifer later lost his faith, and the sword fizzled out at a critical moment and could not penetrate even the crude armour of an Ork warlord.

At the start of each Fight sub-phase in which the wielder is locked in combat, roll a D6 to determine which profile the Monster Slayer of Caliban uses that turn.

D6 — Result

1 *With a fizzle, the ancient runes dim and the sword is indistinguishable from any other power weapon.*

Range	S	AP	Type
-	User	3	Melee

2-4 *The sword powers up and thrums with energy.*

Range	S	AP	Type
-	+1	3	Melee

5-6 *The Monster Slayer is possessed of great strength and matchless killing ability.*

Range	S	AP	Type
-	+2	3	Melee, Instant Death

Shroud of Heroes

The rites of the Dark Angels dictate that when one of their mightiest is slain in glorious battle, his recovered remains are wrapped in a death shroud until he can be interred within the crypts of the Lion's Sanctum deep within the Rock. Pieces of this fabric, stained in the blood of heroes, are then continually fashioned into a single set of robes known as the Shroud of Heroes. It is customary for the Shroud of Heroes to be presented to a noble warrior of the Chapter who will wear it for the duration of a battle or ongoing campaign before passing the revered robes on to another worthy aspirant of the Chapter. Those who wear the Shroud of Heroes claim they can feel the protective powers of their predecessors swirling around them, still eager to aid the Chapter.

The Shroud of Heroes confers the Feel No Pain special rule on its wearer. In addition, while he is not in a unit, he has the Shrouded special rule.

Sons of the Lion

Dark Angels Space Marines are a rewarding army to collect, as they have a plethora of fantastic characters, troops and vehicles at their disposal. The contrast of monastic robes and futuristic power armour is striking, as is the rich body of heraldic colour schemes, icons, banners and tactical markings that the Dark Angels have drawn upon since the founding of the Imperium.

Azrael, Supreme Grand Master of the Dark Angels, accompanied by a mysterious Watcher in the Dark bearing the Lion Helm

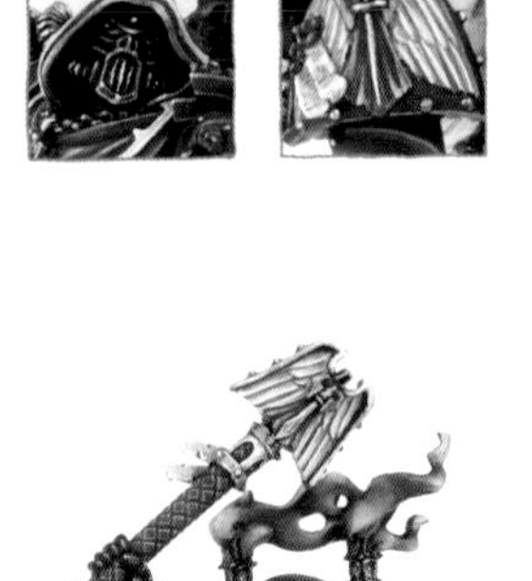

Asmodai, Master Interrogator-Chaplain

Ezekiel, Grand Master of Librarians

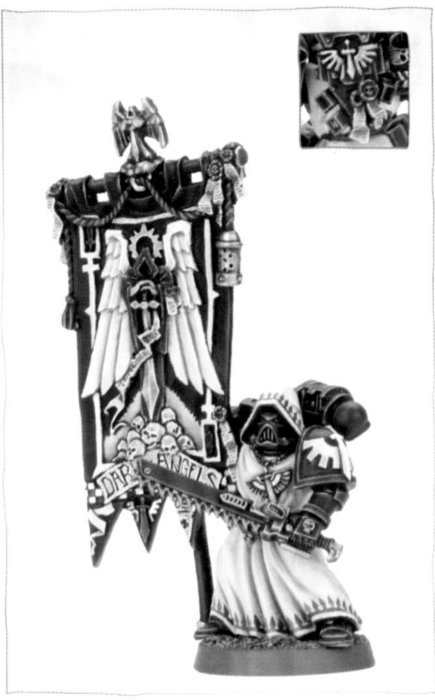

It is a great honour to carry the Dark Angels Chapter Banner into battle.

The three eldest and most treasured of all the Dark Angels' banners are the Sacred Standards. They are (left to right) the Standards of Fortitude, Devastation and Retribution – each a prized heirloom that dates back to the days of the Great Crusade. It is customary for only one of these hallowed standards to be used at any one time: the others are kept in the Great Hall on the Rock.

Chaplain with power fist

Chaplain with plasma pistol

Dark Angels Librarians

Company Master of the 3rd Company

Master Balthasar of the 5th Company

Company Master with plasma pistol and power sword

Ezekiel clears a path for the Company Veterans with a blistering psychic attack.

Company Champion

Apothecary

5th Company Standard Bearer

Veteran Sergeant with bolt pistol and power fist

Veteran with plasma gun

Sergeant with bolt pistol and chainsword

Dark Angels Space Marines with boltguns

Space Marine with plasma cannon

Space Marine with missile launcher

A Dark Angels Tactical Squad from the 5th Company, broken down into a five-man combat squad led by a Veteran Sergeant.

The Dark Angels advance to unleash a storm of vengeance upon the Emperor's foes.

Company Veteran with chainsword and plasma pistol

Company Veteran with plasma pistol and combat shield

Company Veteran with power sword and bolt pistol

Company Veterans with boltguns

Deathwing icon

Ravenwing icon

Dark Angels icon (3rd-10th companies)

1st (Tactical) Squad shoulder markings

2nd (Tactical) Squad shoulder markings

7th (Assault) Squad shoulder markings

9th (Devastator) Squad shoulder markings

Company markings shown on left knee pad

1st

2nd

3rd

4th

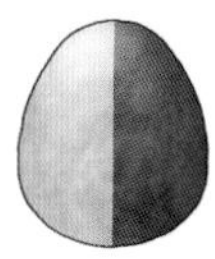

5th

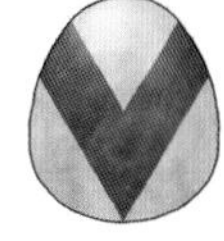

6th

7th

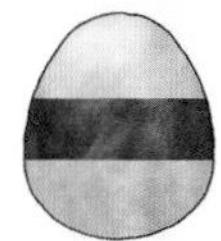

8th

9th

Dark Angels Assault Marines with chainswords and bolt pistols

Assault Marine Sergeant with plasma pistol

Devastator with lascannon

Devastator Sergeant with signum

Devastator with heavy bolter

Devastator with missile launcher

Techmarine with servo-harness

Techmarine with a servo-arm

Servitors assist Techmarines and are equipped with servo-arms, or bear heavy weapons.

Scout with boltgun

Scout Sergeant with bolt pistol and chainsword

Scout with missile launcher

Scouts with sniper rifles and camo cloaks

Dreadnought with assault cannon and missile launcher

Dreadnought with twin-linked lascannon and power fist

Angels of Vengeance Company Veteran

Consecrators Space Marine with boltgun

Angels of Redemption Space Marine

Guardians of the Covenant Company Veteran

Angels of Absolution Space Marine

Disciples of Caliban Space Marine with meltagun

Destructor pattern Predator battle tank

Interior detail showing scanner console and stowed bolter

5th Company Rhino APC, Tactical Squad designation

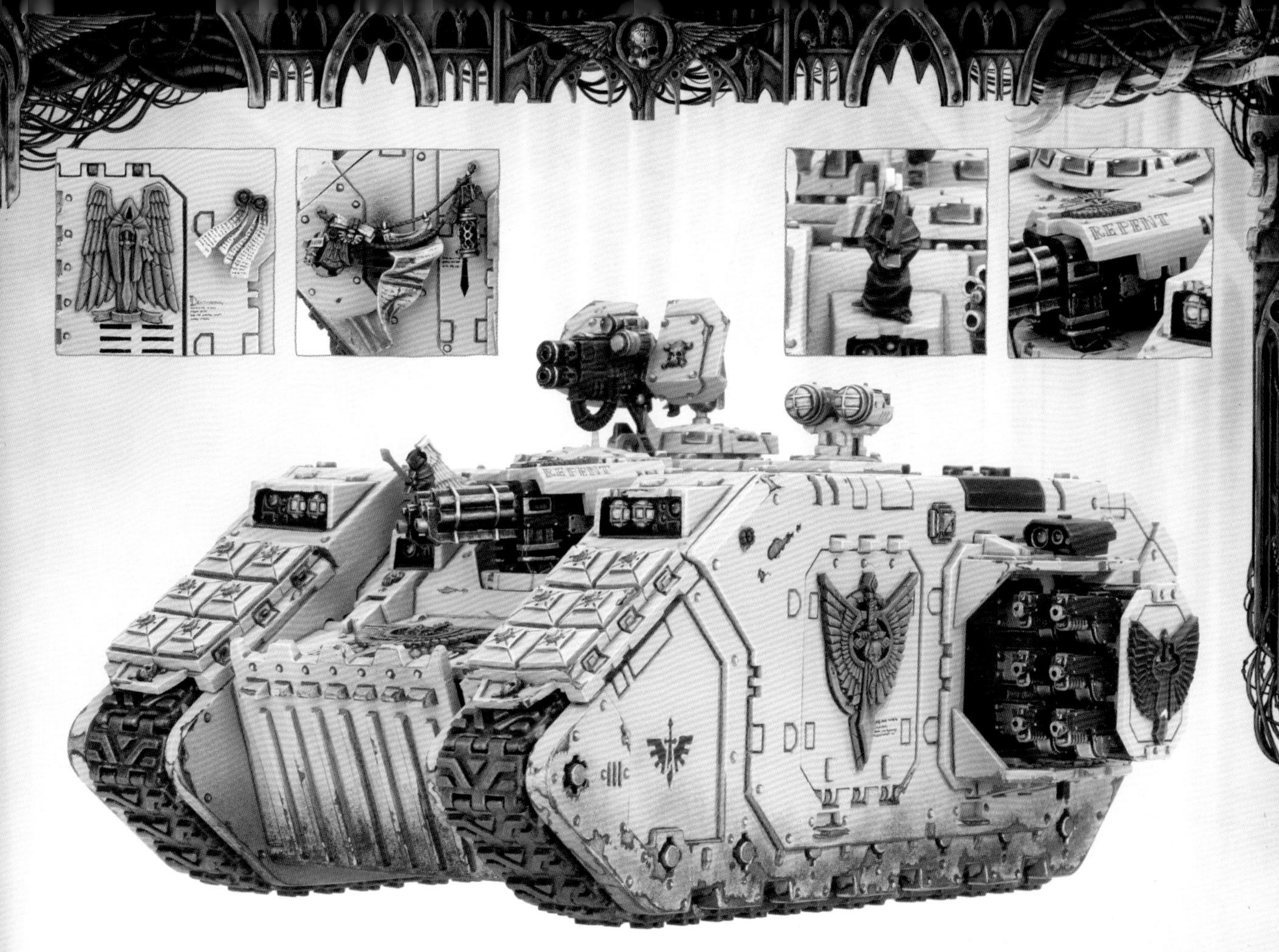

Deathwing Land Raider Crusader

A Deathwing Terminator Squad disembarks from a Land Raider Crusader, ready to unleash the Emperor's judgement.

Belial, Grand Master of the Deathwing

Deathwing Terminator Sergeant with power sword and storm bolter

Deathwing Terminator with cyclone missile launcher and storm bolter

Deathwing Terminator Apothecary

Deathwing Company Champion with the Halberd of Caliban

Watcher in the Dark bearing a Perfidious Relic

Deathwing Terminator with plasma cannon

Deathwing Terminator with lightning claws

Deathwing Terminator carrying the Deathwing Company Banner

Grand Master Belial tirelessly leads the hunt for the Fallen.

Deathwing Knight Master with a flail of the Unforgiven

Deathwing Knight with mace of absolution and storm shield

Deathwing Knights are the finest warriors of the elite 1st Company.

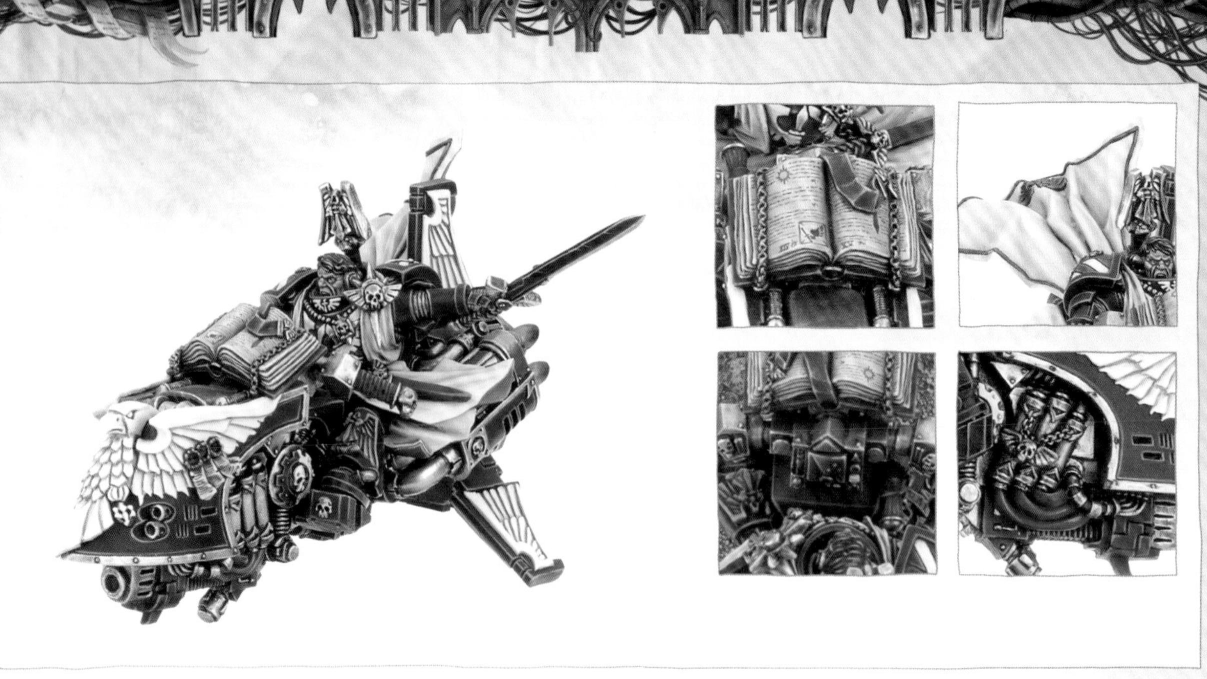

Sammael, Grand Master of the Ravenwing, rides to battle on Corvex, *his jetbike – a sleek, death-dealing marvel preserved from a lost age.*

Ravenwing Champion with a blade of Caliban

Ravenwing Black Knight bearing the Ravenwing Company Banner

Ravenwing Apothecary

Black Knight with Ravenwing grenade launcher

Ravenwing Bikers are masters of swift hit-and-run tactics.

Ravenwing Sergeant with power sword

The cupola of the Darkshroud bears a heavy bolter, but can be upgraded to carry an assault cannon.

The Ravenwing Darkshroud is an ominous icon of the Dark Angels 2nd Company.

Ravenwing Land Speeder with heavy bolter

Typhoon pattern Land Speeder with heavy bolter and typhoon missile launcher

Fast and deadly, this Land Speeder Vengeance mounts a formidable plasma storm battery and an assault cannon.

Rift cannon

The Dark Talon carries a single stasis bomb.

The Ravenwing Dark Talon bristles with weaponry.

Like an angel of death, the Nephilim Jetfighter uses its formidable armament to clear a path for the Ravenwing squadrons.

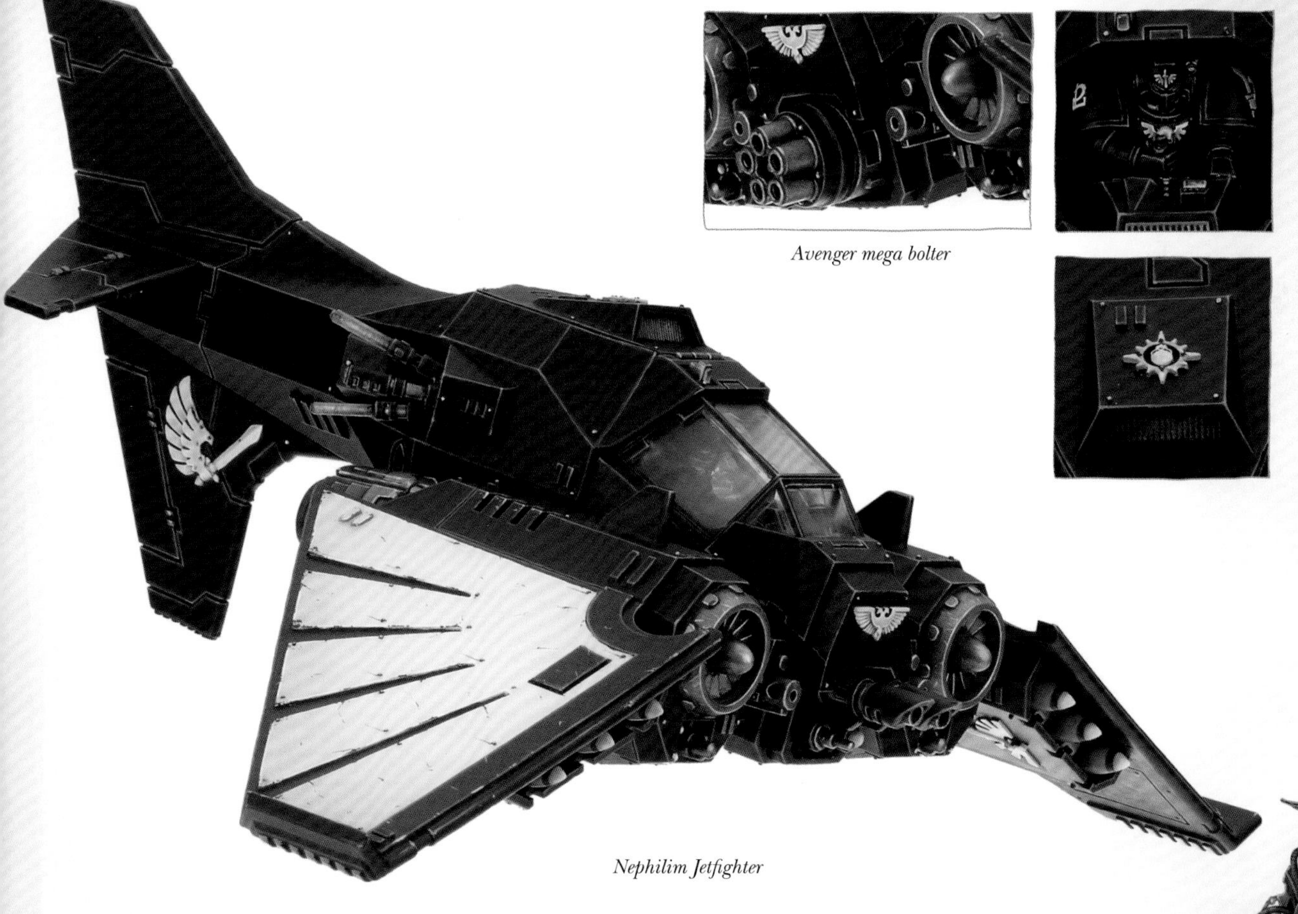

Avenger mega bolter

Nephilim Jetfighter

ANGELS OF DEATH

The following army list enables you to field an army of Dark Angels Space Marines and fight battles using the missions included in the *Warhammer 40,000* rulebook.

USING THE ARMY LIST

The Dark Angels army list is split into six sections: HQ, troops, dedicated transports, elites, fast attack and heavy support. All of the squads, vehicles and characters in the army are placed into one of these categories depending upon their role on the battlefield. Each model is also given a points value, which varies depending on how effective that model is in battle.

Before you choose an army, you will need to agree with your opponent upon the type of game you are going to play and the maximum total number of points each of you will spend. Then you can proceed to pick your army following the guidelines given in the *Warhammer 40,000* rulebook.

ARMY LIST ENTRIES

Each entry in the army list represents a different unit.

More information about the background and rules for the Dark Angels and their options can be found in The Unforgiven section, while examples of the Citadel miniatures you will need to represent them can be found in the Sons of the Lion section.

INTERROGATOR-CHAPLAIN ❶ — ❶ 110 Points

❷	WS	BS	S	T	W	I	A	Ld	Sv	❸ Unit Type	❹ Unit Composition	Page
Interrogator-Chaplain	5	5	4	4	3	5	3	10	3+	Infantry (Character)	1 Interrogator-Chaplain	30

❺ **Wargear:**
- Power armour
- Bolt pistol
- Crozius arcanum
- Frag grenades
- Krak grenades
- Rosarius

❻ **Special Rules:**
- Independent Character
- Inner Circle
- Zealot

❼ **Options:**
- An Interrogator-Chaplain in power armour may take items from the **Melee Weapons**, **Ranged Weapons**, **Special Issue Wargear** and/or **Chapter Relics** sections of the wargear list.
- An Interrogator-Chaplain may replace his power armour, bolt pistol and frag and krak grenades with Terminator armour and a storm bolter .... *30 pts*
  - An Interrogator-Chaplain in Terminator armour may take items

Each unit entry in the Dark Angels army list contains the following information:

❶ **Unit Name:** *At the start of each army list entry you will find the name of the unit alongside the points cost of the unit without any upgrades.*

❷ **Unit Profile:** *This section will show the profile of any models the unit can include, even if they are upgrades.*

❸ **Unit Type:** *This refers to the unit type rules in the* Warhammer 40,000 *rulebook. For example, a unit may be classed as Infantry, Cavalry or Vehicle, which will subject it to a number of rules regarding movement, shooting, assaults, etc.*

❹ **Unit Composition:** *Where applicable, this section will show the number and type of models that make up the basic unit, before any upgrades are taken. If the Unit Composition includes the word 'Unique', then you may only include one of this unit in your army.*

❺ **Wargear:** *This section details the weapons and equipment the models in the unit are armed with. The cost for all these models and their equipment is included in the points cost listed next to the unit name.*

❻ **Special Rules:** *Any special rules that apply to the models in the unit are listed here. These special rules are explained in further detail in either The Unforgiven section of this book or the Special Rules section of the* Warhammer 40,000 *rulebook.*

❼ **Options:** *This section lists all of the upgrades you may add to the unit if you wish to do so, alongside the associated points cost for each. Where an option states that you may exchange one weapon 'and/or' another, you may replace either or both, provided you pay the points cost for each. The abbreviation 'pts' stands for 'points' and 'pts/model' stands for 'points per model'.*

Dedicated Transport: *Where applicable, this option refers to any Transports the unit may take. These have their own army list entries. Dedicated Transports do not use up any Force Organisation chart selections, but otherwise function as separate units. The Transports section of the* Warhammer 40,000 *rulebook explains how Dedicated Transports work.*

Warlord Traits: *Sometimes an entry will have a specific Warlord Trait, in which case it will be listed here in its army list entry.*

Chapter Relics: *Some entries have unique Chapter Relics, listed here. These, like wargear, are already included in the unit's points cost.*

Dark Angels Wargear List

These lists detail the points values of various items of wargear available to units in your army. Many unit entries in the army list that follows may include wargear options from one or more of these lists – in each instance, the army list entry will tell you (in bold text) exactly which of these lists you may use.

Ranged Weapons **.. Page 60**
A model can replace his bolt pistol and/or close combat weapon with one of the following:
- Boltgun .... *free*
- Storm bolter .... *5 pts*
- Combi-flamer, -melta or -plasma .... *10 pts*
- Plasma pistol .... *15 pts*

Melee Weapons **.. Page 62**
A model can replace one weapon with one of the following:
- Chainsword .... *free*
- Lightning claw .... *15 pts*
- Power weapon .... *15 pts*
- Power fist .... *25 pts*
- Thunder hammer .... *30 pts*

Terminator Weapons
A model wearing Terminator armour can replace his storm bolter with one of the following:
- Combi-flamer, -melta or -plasma .... *6 pts*

Special Issue Wargear **.. Page 63**
A model can take up to one of each of the following:
- Auspex .... *5 pts*
- Combat shield .... *5 pts*
- Infravisor .... *5 pts*
- Melta bombs .... *5 pts*
- Digital weapons .... *10 pts*
- Porta-rack .... *10 pts*
- Conversion field .... *15 pts*
- Jump pack [1, 3] .... *15 pts*
- Space Marine bike [1, 2] .... *20 pts*
- Displacer field .... *25 pts*
- Power field generator .... *30 pts*

Chapter Relics **.. Page 67**
Only one of each Relic may be taken per army.
A model can replace one weapon with one of the following.
- Foe-smiter .... *20 pts*
- Lion's Roar .... *20 pts*
- Mace of Redemption .... *30 pts*
- Monster Slayer of Caliban .... *45 pts*
- Shroud of Heroes* .... *50 pts*

** Does not replace one of the character's weapons*

Sacred Standards **.. Page 66**
You may only include one Sacred Standard per army.
A standard bearer can take one of the following:
- Standard of Retribution .... *45 pts*
- Standard of Devastation .... *65 pts*
- Standard of Fortitude .... *85 pts*

Dark Angels Vehicle Equipment **........................ Page 65**
A model can take up to one of each of the following:
- Dozer blade .... *5 pts*
- Storm bolter .... *5 pts*
- Extra armour .... *10 pts*
- Hunter-killer missile .... *10 pts*

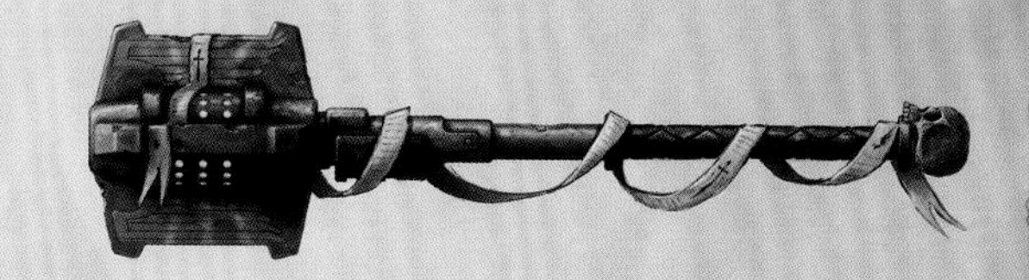

Notes

[1] May not be taken by models wearing Terminator armour. Note that these pieces of wargear are mutually exclusive. For example, a Librarian riding a Space Marine bike may not also take a jump pack.
[2] May not be taken by a Company Master.
[3] May not be taken by a Techmarine.

HQ

AZRAEL

215 Points

	WS	BS	S	T	W	I	A	Ld	Sv	Unit Type	Unit Composition	Page
Azrael	6	5	4	4	4	5	4	10	2+	Infantry (Character)	1 (Unique)	52

Wargear:
- Frag grenades
- Krak grenades

Chapter Relics:
- Protector
- Lion's Wrath
- Sword of Secrets
- Lion Helm

Warlord Trait:
- If Azrael is in your army, he must be your Warlord. He can choose any one of the Dark Angels Warlord Traits (there is no need to roll).

Special Rules:
- Independent Character
- Inner Circle
- Rites of Battle

Supreme Grand Master of the Dark Angels:
In a primary detachment that contains Azrael, Ravenwing Attack Squadrons and Deathwing Terminator Squads are troops choices instead of their usual Force Organisation categories.

EZEKIEL

145 Points

	WS	BS	S	T	W	I	A	Ld	Sv	Unit Type	Unit Composition	Page
Ezekiel	5	5	4	4	3	5	3	10	2+	Infantry (Character)	1 (Unique)	54

Wargear:
- Artificer armour
- Master-crafted bolt pistol
- Frag grenades
- Krak grenades
- Psychic hood

Chapter Relics:
- Traitor's Bane
- Book of Salvation

Warlord Trait:
- The Hunt

Special Rules:
- Independent Character
- Inner Circle
- Psyker (Mastery Level 3)

Psyker:
Ezekiel always knows the *Mind Worm* psychic power. He may generate two more powers from the **Divination**, **Pyromancy**, **Telepathy** and **Telekinesis** disciplines.

ASMODAI

140 Points

	WS	BS	S	T	W	I	A	Ld	Sv	Unit Type	Unit Composition	Page
Asmodai	5	5	4	4	3	5	3	10	3+	Infantry (Character)	1 (Unique)	55

Wargear:
- Power armour
- Crozius arcanum
- Frag grenades
- Krak grenades
- Rosarius

Chapter Relic:
- Blades of Reason

Warlord Trait:
- The Hunt

Special Rules:
- Fear
- Independent Character
- Inner Circle
- Zealot

BELIAL

190 Points

	WS	BS	S	T	W	I	A	Ld	Sv	Unit Type	Unit Composition	Page
Belial	6	5	4	4	3	5	3	10	2+	Infantry (Character)	1 (Unique)	56

Wargear:
- Terminator armour
- Storm bolter
- Teleport homer

Chapter Relic:
- Sword of Silence

Warlord Trait:
- The Hunt

Special Rules:
- Deathwing Assault
- Independent Character
- Inner Circle
- Marked for Retribution
- Tactical Precision
- Vengeful Strike

Options:
- Replace storm bolter and Sword of Silence with thunder hammer and storm shield.................................... *free*
- Replace storm bolter and Sword of Silence with a pair of lighting claws.................................... *free*

Grand Master of the Deathwing:
In a primary detachment that contains Belial, Deathwing Terminator Squads are troops choices instead of elites choices.

HQ

SAMMAEL — 200 Points

	WS	BS	S	T	W	I	A	Ld	Sv	Unit Type	Unit Composition	Page
Sammael	6	5	4	5	3	5	3	10	3+	Jetbike (Character)	1 (Unique)	58

Wargear:
- Power armour
- Bolt pistol
- Frag and krak grenades
- Teleport homer

Chapter Relics:
- Raven Sword
- Adamantine Mantle
- Corvex
- Night Halo

Warlord Trait:
- Rapid Manoeuvre

Special Rules:
- Hit & Run
- Independent Character
- Inner Circle
- Scouts
- Skilled Rider

Options:
- May replace *Corvex* with the Grand Master of the Ravenwing's Land Speeder, *Sableclaw,* at no additional points cost, in which case the unit type is changed to Vehicle (Fast, Skimmer).

Grand Master of the Ravenwing:
In a primary detachment that contains Sammael, Ravenwing Attack Squadrons are troops choices instead of fast attack choices.

	Armour					Unit Type	Unit Composition	Page
	BS	F	S	R	HP			
Sableclaw	5	14	14	10	2	Vehicle (Fast, Skimmer)	1 (Unique)	58

Wargear:
- Twin-linked assault cannon
- Twin-linked heavy bolter

Chapter Relic:
- Night Halo

Special Rules:
- Deep Strike

COMPANY MASTER — 90 Points

	WS	BS	S	T	W	I	A	Ld	Sv	Unit Type	Unit Composition	Page
Company Master	6	5	4	4	3	5	3	10	3+	Infantry (Character)	1 Company Master	29

Wargear:
- Power armour
- Bolt pistol
- Chainsword
- Frag grenades
- Krak grenades
- Iron halo

Special Rules:
- Independent Character
- Inner Circle

Options:
- May take a storm shield .... *15 pts*
- May take a Perfidious Relic of the Unforgiven .... *15 pts*
- May replace power armour with artificer armour .... *20 pts*
  - A Company Master in power armour or artificer armour may take items from the **Melee Weapons**, **Ranged Weapons**, **Special Issue Wargear** and/or **Chapter Relics** sections of the wargear list.
- A Company Master may replace his power armour, bolt pistol, chainsword, frag and krak grenades with Terminator armour, storm bolter and power sword .... *40 pts*
  - A Company Master in Terminator armour may take items from the **Terminator Weapons**, **Special Issue Wargear** and/or **Chapter Relics** sections of the wargear list.

INTERROGATOR-CHAPLAIN — 110 Points

	WS	BS	S	T	W	I	A	Ld	Sv	Unit Type	Unit Composition	Page
Interrogator-Chaplain	5	5	4	4	3	5	3	10	3+	Infantry (Character)	1 Interrogator-Chaplain	30

Wargear:
- Power armour
- Bolt pistol
- Crozius arcanum
- Frag grenades
- Krak grenades
- Rosarius

Special Rules:
- Independent Character
- Inner Circle
- Zealot

Options:
- An Interrogator-Chaplain in power armour may take items from the **Melee Weapons**, **Ranged Weapons**, **Special Issue Wargear** and/or **Chapter Relics** sections of the wargear list.
- An Interrogator-Chaplain may replace his power armour, bolt pistol and frag and krak grenades with Terminator armour and a storm bolter .... *30 pts*
  - An Interrogator-Chaplain in Terminator armour may take items from the **Terminator Weapons**, **Special Issue Wargear** and/or **Chapter Relics** sections of the wargear list.

HQ

CHAPLAIN

90 Points

	WS	BS	S	T	W	I	A	Ld	Sv	Unit Type	Unit Composition	Page
Chaplain	5	4	4	4	2	4	2	10	3+	Infantry (Character)	1 Chaplain	30

Wargear:
- Power armour
- Bolt pistol
- Crozius arcanum
- Frag grenades
- Krak grenades
- Rosarius

Special Rules:
- Independent Character
- Zealot

Options:
- May take items from the **Melee Weapons**, **Ranged Weapons** and/or **Special Issue Wargear** sections of the wargear list.

LIBRARIAN

65 Points

	WS	BS	S	T	W	I	A	Ld	Sv	Unit Type	Unit Composition	Page
Librarian	5	4	4	4	2	4	2	10	3+	Infantry (Character)	1 Librarian	31

Wargear:
- Power armour
- Bolt pistol
- Force weapon
- Frag grenades
- Krak grenades
- Psychic hood

Special Rules:
- Independent Character
- Inner Circle
- Psyker (Mastery Level 1)

Psyker:
Dark Angels Librarians are Psykers who use the **Divination**, **Pyromancy**, **Telepathy**, and **Telekinesis** disciplines.

Options:
- May upgrade to Psyker (Mastery Level 2)..*35 pts*
- A Librarian in power armour may take items from the **Melee Weapons**, **Ranged Weapons**, **Special Issue Wargear** and/or **Chapter Relics** sections of the wargear list.
- A Librarian may replace his power armour, bolt pistol and frag and krak grenades with Terminator armour and storm bolter ....*30 pts*
  - A Librarian in Terminator armour may only take items from the **Terminator Weapons**, **Special Issue Wargear** and/or **Chapter Relics** sections of the wargear list.

TECHMARINE

50 Points

For each HQ choice in your army (not including other Techmarines or Command Squads of any type) you may include a Techmarine. These selections do not use up a Force Organisation slot.

	WS	BS	S	T	W	I	A	Ld	Sv	Unit Type	Unit Composition	Page
Techmarine	4	4	4	4	1	4	1	8	2+	Infantry (Character)	1 Techmarine	32

Wargear:
- Artificer armour
- Bolt pistol
- Servo-arm
- Frag grenades
- Krak grenades

Special Rules:
- And They Shall Know No Fear
- Blessing of the Omnissiah
- Bolster Defences
- Grim Resolve
- Independent Character

Options:
- May upgrade servo-arm to servo-harness..*25 pts*
- May take items from the **Melee Weapons**, **Ranged Weapons** and/or **Special Issue Wargear** sections of the wargear list.

SERVITORS

10 Points

You may include one unit of Servitors for each Techmarine in your army. They do not take up a Forge Organisation slot.

	WS	BS	S	T	W	I	A	Ld	Sv	Unit Type	Unit Composition	Page
Servitor	3	3	3	3	1	3	1	8	4+	Infantry	1 Servitor	32

Wargear:
- Servo-arm

Special Rules:
- Mindlock

Options:
- May include up to four additional Servitors..*10 pts/model*
- Up to two Servitors may replace their servo-arm with a:
  - Heavy bolter or multi-melta..*10 pts/model*
  - Plasma cannon..*20 pts/model*

HQ

COMMAND SQUAD

100 Points

For each HQ choice in your army (not including Techmarines or other Command Squads of any type) you may include a Command Squad. These selections do not use up a Force Organisation slot.

	WS	BS	S	T	W	I	A	Ld	Sv	Unit Type	Unit Composition	Page
Veteran	4	4	4	4	1	4	2	9	3+	Infantry	5 Veterans	33
Company Champion	5	4	4	4	1	4	2	9	3+	Infantry (Character)		
Apothecary	4	4	4	4	1	4	2	9	3+	Infantry (Character)		

Wargear:
- Power armour
- Bolt pistol
- Chainsword
- Frag grenades
- Krak grenades

Special Rules:
- And They Shall Know No Fear
- Grim Resolve

Options:
- One Veteran may take a banner from the following list:
  - Company Standard....................................*15 pts*
  - Revered Standard....................................*25 pts*
  - Dark Angels Chapter Banner*....................*45 pts*
  - Alternatively, they may take a banner from the **Sacred Standards** section of the wargear list.
- One Veteran may be upgraded to a Company Champion, replacing their chainsword with a blade of Caliban and a combat shield..........*15 pts*
- One Veteran may be upgraded to an Apothecary, replacing their bolt pistol with a narthecium ....*15 pts*

* *One per army*

- Any Veteran may replace his bolt pistol with a plasma pistol..............................*15 pts/model*
- Any Veteran may take:
  - Melta bombs ....*5 pts/model*
  - Storm shield..*15 pts/model*
- Any Veteran may replace his chainsword and/or bolt pistol with a:
  - Bolter ....*free*
  - Storm bolter..*3 pts/model*
  - Flamer ....*5 pts/model*
  - Meltagun ....*10 pts/model*
  - Combi-flamer, -melta, or -plasma ....*10 pts/model*
  - Plasma gun, power weapon or lightning claw ....*15 pts/model*
  - Power fist..*25 pts/model*
  - Thunder hammer...................................*30 pts/model*
- May select a Drop Pod, Rhino, or Razorback as a Dedicated Transport (pg 100).

DEATHWING COMMAND SQUAD

220 Points

For each HQ choice in your army equipped with Terminator armour (including Belial, but not other Deathwing Command Squads) you may include a Deathwing Command Squad. These selections do not use up a Force Organisation slot.

	WS	BS	S	T	W	I	A	Ld	Sv	Unit Type	Unit Composition	Page
Deathwing Terminator	4	4	4	4	1	4	2	9	2+	Infantry	5 Deathwing Terminators	45
Deathwing Apothecary	4	4	4	4	1	4	2	9	2+	Infantry (Character)		
Deathwing Champion	5	4	4	4	1	4	2	9	2+	Infantry (Character)		

Wargear:
- Terminator armour
- Storm bolter
- Power fist

Special Rules:
- Deathwing Assault
- Inner Circle
- Split Fire
- Vengeful Strike

Options:
- One Deathwing Terminator may take a banner from the following list:
  - Deathwing Company Banner* ....*45 pts*
  - Revered Standard..*20 pts*
  - Alternatively, they may take a banner from the **Sacred Standards** section of the wargear list.
- One Deathwing Terminator may be upgraded to the Deathwing Champion, replacing all of their weapons with the Halberd of Caliban..*5 pts*
- One Deathwing Terminator may be upgraded to a Deathwing Apothecary, replacing their power fist with a narthecium ....*30 pts*

* *One per army*

- One Deathwing Terminator may choose one of the following options:
  - o take a cyclone missile launcher....................*25 pts*
  - o replace his storm bolter with:
    - a heavy flamer ....*10 pts*
    - a plasma cannon ....*15 pts*
    - an assault cannon..*20 pts*
- Any Deathwing Terminator may replace all of his weapons with:
  - a pair of lightning claws ....*free*
  - a thunder hammer and storm shield... *5 pts/model*
- Any model may replace his power fist with a chainfist.. *5 pts/model*
- The unit may select a Land Raider of any type as a Dedicated Transport (pg 104). This vehicle must be given the Deathwing Vehicle upgrade at additional cost.

RAVENWING COMMAND SQUAD — 120 Points

For each HQ choice in your army that is mounted on a bike (or Sammael, but not including other Ravenwing Command Squads) you may include a Ravenwing Command Squad. These selections do not use up a Force Organisation slot.

	WS	BS	S	T	W	I	A	Ld	Sv	Unit Type	Unit Composition	Page
Ravenwing Black Knight	4	4	4	5	1	4	2	9	3+	Bike	3 Ravenwing Black Knights	47
Ravenwing Apothecary	4	4	4	5	1	4	2	9	3+	Bike (Character)		
Ravenwing Champion	5	4	4	5	1	4	2	9	3+	Bike (Character)		

Wargear:
- Power armour
- Bolt pistol
- Plasma talon
- Corvus hammer
- Frag grenades
- Krak grenades
- Teleport homer

Special Rules:
- And They Shall Know No Fear
- Grim Resolve
- Hit & Run
- Scouts
- Skilled Rider

Options:
- One Ravenwing Black Knight may take a banner from the following list:
  - Ravenwing Company Banner* .... *15 pts*
  - Revered Standard .... *25 pts*
  - Alternatively, they may take a banner from the **Relic Banners** section of the wargear list.
- One Ravenwing Black Knight may replace his plasma talon with a Ravenwing grenade launcher .... *free*
- One Ravenwing Black Knight may be upgraded to a Ravenwing Apothecary, replacing their bolt pistol with a narthecium .... *30 pts*
- One Ravenwing Black Knight in the army may be upgraded to the Ravenwing Champion, replacing his corvus hammer with a blade of Caliban .... *5 pts*

* *One per army*

TROOPS

TACTICAL SQUAD — 70 Points

	WS	BS	S	T	W	I	A	Ld	Sv	Unit Type	Unit Composition	Page
Space Marine	4	4	4	4	1	4	1	8	3+	Infantry	4 Space Marines	35
Space Marine Sergeant	4	4	4	4	1	4	1	8	3+	Infantry (Character)	1 Space Marine Sergeant	
Veteran Sergeant	4	4	4	4	1	4	2	9	3+	Infantry (Character)		

Wargear:
- Power armour
- Boltgun
- Bolt pistol
- Frag grenades
- Krak grenades

Special Rules:
- And They Shall Know No Fear
- Combat Squads
- Grim Resolve

Options:
- May include up to five additional Space Marines .... *14 pts/model*
- If the squad numbers less than ten models, one Space Marine may replace his boltgun with *either* a special *or* heavy weapon from the list, right.
- If the squad numbers ten models, one Space Marine may replace his boltgun with a special weapon, *and* one Space Marine may replace his boltgun with a heavy weapon from the list, right.
- May upgrade the Space Marine Sergeant to a Veteran Sergeant.................................... *10 pts*
- The Space Marine Sergeant or Veteran Sergeant may take items from the **Melee Weapons** and/or **Ranged Weapons** sections of the wargear list.
- The Space Marine Sergeant or Veteran Sergeant may take melta bombs.......... *5 pts*
- May select a Drop Pod, Rhino, or Razorback as a Dedicated Transport (pg 100).

Special Weapons:
- Flamer .... *5 pts*
- Meltagun .... *10 pts*
- Plasma gun .... *15 pts*

Heavy Weapons:
- Heavy bolter.. *10 pts*
- Multi-melta... *10 pts*
- Missile launcher (with frag and krak missiles) .... *15 pts*
  - May also take flakk missiles .... *10 pts*
- Plasma cannon.. *15 pts*
- Lascannon... *20 pts*

SCOUT SQUAD — 60 Points

	WS	BS	S	T	W	I	A	Ld	Sv	Unit Type	Unit Composition	Page
Scout	3	3	4	4	1	4	1	8	4+	Infantry	4 Scouts	37
Scout Sergeant	4	4	4	4	1	4	1	8	4+	Infantry (Character)	1 Scout Sergeant	
Veteran Scout Sergeant	4	4	4	4	1	4	2	9	4+	Infantry (Character)		

Wargear:
- Scout armour
- Boltgun
- Bolt pistol
- Frag grenades
- Krak grenades

Special Rules:
- And They Shall Know No Fear
- Combat Squads
- Infiltrate
- Move Through Cover
- Scouts

Options:
- May include up to five additional Scouts.................................. *12 pts/model*
- The squad can have camo cloaks .... *2 pts/model*
- Any model may replace his boltgun with a Space Marine shotgun, combat knife or sniper rifle... *free*
- One Scout may replace his boltgun with one of the following:
  - Heavy bolter.. *8 pts*
  - Missile launcher (with frag and krak missiles) .... *15 pts*
    - May also take flakk missiles .... *10 pts*
- May upgrade the Scout Sergeant to a Veteran Scout Sergeant................................ *10 pts*
- The Scout Sergeant or Veteran Scout Sergeant may take items from the **Melee Weapons** and/or **Ranged Weapons** sections of the wargear list.
- The Scout Sergeant or Veteran Scout Sergeant may take melta bombs .... *5 pts*

Elites

COMPANY VETERANS SQUAD — 90 Points

	WS	BS	S	T	W	I	A	Ld	Sv	Unit Type	Unit Composition	Page
Veteran	4	4	4	4	1	4	2	9	3+	Infantry	4 Veteran Space Marines	36
Veteran Sergeant	4	4	4	4	1	4	2	9	3+	Infantry (Character)	1 Veteran Sergeant	

Wargear:
- Power armour
- Boltgun
- Bolt pistol
- Frag grenades
- Krak grenades

Special Rules:
- And They Shall Know No Fear
- Combat Squads
- Grim Resolve

Options:
- May include up to five additional Veterans .... *18 pts/ model*
- Any model may replace his boltgun with a chainsword .... *free*
- Up to three models may replace their boltguns with one of the following:
  - Storm bolter .... *5 pts/model*
  - Combi-weapon .... *10 pts/model*
  - Power weapon, lightning claw or plasma pistol .... *15 pts/model*
  - Power fist .... *25 pts/model*
  - Pair of lightning claws .... *30 pts/model*
- Any model may take:
  - Combat shield .... *5 pts/model*
  - Melta bombs .... *5 pts/model*
  - Storm shield .... *10 pts/model*
- For every full five models in the squad, one Veteran may replace his boltgun with one of the following:
  - Flamer .... *5 pts/model*
  - Meltagun .... *10 pts/model*
  - Plasma gun .... *15 pts/model*
- One Veteran can replace his boltgun with one of the following:
  - Heavy bolter .... *10 pts*
  - Multi-melta .... *10 pts*
  - Missile launcher (with frag and krak missiles) .... *15 pts*
    - May also take flakk missiles .... *10 pts*
  - Plasma cannon .... *15 pts*
  - Lascannon .... *20 pts*
- May select a Drop Pod, Rhino, or Razorback as a Dedicated Transport (pg 100).

Elites

DEATHWING TERMINATOR SQUAD — 220 Points

	WS	BS	S	T	W	I	A	Ld	Sv	Unit Type	Unit Composition	Page
Deathwing Terminator	4	4	4	4	1	4	2	9	2+	Infantry	4 Deathwing Terminators	44
Deathwing Term Sgt.	4	4	4	4	1	4	2	9	2+	Infantry (Character)	1 Deathwing Terminator Sergeant	

Wargear:
- Terminator armour
- Storm bolter
- Power fist (Deathwing Terminator only)
- Power sword (Deathwing Term Sergeant only)

Special Rules:
- Deathwing Assault
- Inner Circle
- Split Fire
- Vengeful Strike

Options:
- May include up to five additional Deathwing Terminators .... *44 pts/model*
- Any model can replace all of his weapons with:
  - Pair of lightning claws .... *free*
  - Thunder hammer and storm shield .... *5 pts/model*
- Any model can replace his power fist with a chainfist .... *5 pts/model*
- For every five models in the squad, one Deathwing Terminator may choose one of the following options:
  - Replace his storm bolter with a heavy flamer .... *10 pts/model*
  - Replace his storm bolter with a plasma cannon .... *15 pts/model*
  - Replace his storm bolter with an assault cannon .... *20 pts/model*
  - Take a cyclone missile launcher .... *25 pts/model*
- Deathwing Terminator Squads may select a Land Raider of any type as a Dedicated Transport (pg 104). This vehicle must be given the Deathwing Vehicle upgrade at additional cost.

DEATHWING KNIGHTS — 235 Points

	WS	BS	S	T	W	I	A	Ld	Sv	Unit Type	Unit Composition	Page
Deathwing Knight	5	4	4	4	1	4	2	9	2+	Infantry	4 Deathwing Knights	45
Knight Master	5	4	4	4	1	4	3	9	2+	Infantry (Character)	1 Knight Master	

Wargear:
- Terminator armour
- Flail of the Unforgiven (Knight Master only)
- Mace of absolution (Deathwing Knight only)
- Storm shield

Special Rules:
- Deathwing Assault
- Fortress of Shields
- Hammer of Wrath
- Inner Circle
- You Cannot Hide

Options:
- May include up to five additional Deathwing Knights .... *46 pts/model*
- May take a Perfidious Relic of the Unforgiven (pg 64) .... *10 pts*
- Deathwing Knights may select a Land Raider of any type as a Dedicated Transport (pg 104). This vehicle must be given the Deathwing Vehicle upgrade at additional cost.

DREADNOUGHT — 100 Points

	WS	BS	S	Armour F	Armour S	Armour R	I	A	HP	Unit Type	Unit Composition	Page
Dreadnought	4	4	6	12	12	10	4	2	3	Vehicle (Walker)	1 Dreadnought	43
Venerable Dreadnought	5	5	6	12	12	10	4	2	3	Vehicle (Walker)		43

Wargear:
- Power fist with built-in storm bolter
- Multi-melta
- Searchlight
- Smoke launchers

Special Rules:
- Deathwing Vehicle (Venerable Dreadnought only)

Options:
- May replace its multi-melta with one of the following:
  - Twin-linked autocannon .... *5 pts*
  - Twin-linked heavy bolter .... *5 pts*
  - Twin-linked heavy flamer .... *5 pts*
  - Plasma cannon .... *10 pts*
  - Assault cannon .... *20 pts*
  - Twin-linked lascannon .... *25 pts*
- May replace storm bolter with heavy flamer .... *10 pts*
- May take extra armour .... *10 pts*
- May replace power fist (and storm bolter) with one of the following
  - missile launcher .... *10 pts*
  - twin-linked autocannon .... *15 pts*
- May upgrade to Venerable Dreadnought .... *25 pts*
- May select a Drop Pod as a Dedicated Transport (pg 100).

Dedicated Transports

RHINO — 35 Points

	BS	Armour F	Armour S	Armour R	HP	Unit Type	Unit Composition	Page
Rhino	4	11	11	10	3	Vehicle (Tank, Transport)	1 Rhino	38

Wargear:
- Storm bolter
- Searchlight
- Smoke launchers

Special Rules:
- Repair

Transport Capacity:
- Ten models

Options:
- Rhinos may take items from the **Dark Angels Vehicle Equipment** list.

RAZORBACK — 55 Points

	BS	Armour F	Armour S	Armour R	HP	Unit Type	Unit Composition	Page
Razorback	4	11	11	10	3	Vehicle (Tank, Transport)	1 Razorback	39

Wargear:
- Twin-linked heavy bolter
- Searchlight
- Smoke launchers

Transport Capacity:
- Six models

Options:
- Razorbacks may take items from the **Dark Angels Vehicle Equipment** list.
- May replace its twin-linked heavy bolter with one of the following:
  - Twin-linked heavy flamer .... *free*
  - Twin-linked assault cannon .... *20 pts*
  - Twin-linked lascannon .... *20 pts*
  - Lascannon and twin-linked plasma gun .... *20 pts*

DROP POD — 35 Points

	BS	Armour F	Armour S	Armour R	HP	Unit Type	Unit Composition	Page
Drop Pod	4	12	12	12	3	Vehicle (Open-topped, Transport)	1 Drop Pod	42

Wargear:
- Storm bolter

Special Rules:
- Drop Pod Assault
- Immobile
- Inertial Guidance System

Transport Capacity:
- Ten models or one Dreadnought

Options:
- May replace its storm bolter with a deathwind launcher .... *15 pts*
- May take a locator beacon .... *10 pts*

Fast Attack

RAVENWING ATTACK SQUADRON — 80 Points

	WS	BS	S	T	W	I	A	Ld	Sv	Unit Type	Unit Composition	Page
Ravenwing Biker	4	4	4	5	1	4	1	8	3+	Bike	2 Ravenwing Bikers	47
Ravenwing Sergeant	4	4	4	5	1	4	1	8	3+	Bike (Character)	1 Ravenwing Sergeant	
Ravenwing Vet. Sergeant	4	4	4	5	1	4	2	9	3+	Bike (Character)		
Ravenwing Attack Bike	4	4	4	5	2	4	2	8	3+	Bike		

Wargear:
- Power armour
- Bolt pistol
- Twin-linked boltgun
- Heavy bolter (Attack Bike only)
- Frag grenades
- Krak grenades
- Teleport homer

Special Rules:
- And They Shall Know No Fear
- Grim Resolve
- Hit & Run
- Ravenwing Combat Squads
- Scouts

Options:
- The squadron may include up to three additional Ravenwing Bikers .... *27 pts/model*
- Any model can replace his bolt pistol with a chainsword .... *free*
- Up to two Ravenwing Bikers may take one of the following:
  - Flamer .... *5 pts/model*
  - Meltagun .... *10 pts/model*
  - Plasma gun .... *15 pts/model*
- The Ravenwing Sergeant may be upgraded to a Ravenwing Veteran Sergeant .... *10 pts*
  - The Ravenwing Sergeant or Veteran Sergeant may take items from the **Melee Weapons** and/or **Ranged Weapons** sections of the wargear list.
  - The Ravenwing Sergeant or Veteran Sergeant may take melta bombs .... *5 pts*
- The squadron may include one Ravenwing Attack Bike .... *45 pts*
  - The Attack Bike can replace its heavy bolter with a multi-melta .... *10 pts*
- If the squadron includes six Ravenwing Bikers (including a Sergeant or Veteran Sergeant), it may include a single Land Speeder chosen from the Ravenwing Support Squadron entry below.

RAVENWING SUPPORT SQUADRON — 50 Points

	BS	Armour F	Armour S	Armour R	HP	Unit Type	Unit Composition	Page
Land Speeder	4	10	10	10	2	Vehicle (Fast, Skimmer)	1 Land Speeder	48

Wargear:
- Heavy bolter

Special Rules:
- Deep Strike

Options:
- Squadron may include up to four additional Land Speeders .... *50 pts/model*
- May replace its heavy bolter with:
  - Heavy flamer .... *free*
  - Multi-melta .... *10 pts/model*
- Any Land Speeder may be upgraded to one of the following:
  - Typhoon pattern with Typhoon missile launcher .... *25 pts/model*
  - Tornado pattern with one of the following:
    - Heavy bolter .... *10 pts/model*
    - Heavy flamer .... *10 pts/model*
    - Multi-melta .... *20 pts/model*
    - Assault cannon .... *30 pts/model*

RAVENWING BLACK KNIGHTS — 126 Points

	WS	BS	S	T	W	I	A	Ld	Sv	Unit Type	Unit Composition	Page
Ravenwing Black Knight	4	4	4	5	1	4	2	9	3+	Bike	2 Ravenwing Black Knights	47
Ravenwing Huntmaster	4	4	4	5	1	4	2	9	3+	Bike (Character)	1 Ravenwing Huntmaster	

Wargear:
- Power armour
- Bolt pistol
- Plasma talon
- Corvus hammer
- Frag grenades
- Krak grenades
- Teleport homer

Special Rules:
- And They Shall Know No Fear
- Grim Resolve
- Hit & Run
- Scouts
- Skilled Rider

Options:
- The squadron may include up to seven additional Ravenwing Black Knights .... *42 pts/model*
- For every full three models in the unit, one Ravenwing Black Knight can replace his plasma talon with a Ravenwing grenade launcher .... *free*
- The Ravenwing Huntmaster may replace his corvus hammer with a power weapon .... *12 pts*
- The Ravenwing Huntmaster may take melta bombs .... *5 pts*

FAST ATTACK

RAVENWING DARKSHROUD — 80 Points

	Armour BS	F	S	R	HP	Unit Type	Unit Composition	Page
Ravenwing Darkshroud	4	10	10	10	2	Vehicle (Fast, Skimmer)	1 Ravenwing Darkshroud	49

Wargear:
- Heavy bolter

Special Rules:
- Deep Strike
- Icon of Old Caliban
- Scouts
- Shroud of Angels
- Stealth

Options:
- May replace its heavy bolter with an assault cannon............*20 pts*

ASSAULT SQUAD — 85 Points

	WS	BS	S	T	W	I	A	Ld	Sv	Unit Type	Unit Composition	Page
Space Marine	4	4	4	4	1	4	1	8	3+	Jump Infantry	4 Space Marines	35
Space Marine Sergeant	4	4	4	4	1	4	1	8	3+	Jump Infantry (Character)	1 Space Marine Sergeant	
Veteran Sergeant	4	4	4	4	1	4	2	9	3+	Jump Infantry (Character)		

Wargear:
- Power armour
- Bolt pistol
- Chainsword
- Frag grenades
- Krak grenades
- Jump pack

Special Rules:
- And They Shall Know No Fear
- Combat Squads
- Grim Resolve

Options:
- May include up to five additional Space Marines ...... *17 pts/model*
- Up to two Space Marines may replace their bolt pistol with a:
  - flamer .... *5 pts/model*
  - plasma pistol .... *15 pts/model*
- May upgrade the Space Marine Sergeant to a Veteran Sergeant..*10 pts*
- The Space Marine Sergeant or Veteran Sergeant may take items from the **Melee Weapons** and/or **Ranged Weapons** sections of the wargear list.
- The Space Marine Sergeant or Veteran Sergeant may take melta bombs ....*5 pts*
- The entire squad may remove their jump packs, changing their unit type to **Infantry**. They may then have a Drop Pod or Rhino for free (pg 100).

NEPHILIM JETFIGHTER — 180 Points

	Armour BS	F	S	R	HP	Unit Type	Unit Composition	Page
Nephilim Jetfighter	4	11	11	11	3	Vehicle (Flyer)	1 Nephilim Jetfighter	50

Wargear:
- Twin-linked heavy bolter
- Twin-linked lascannon
- Six blacksword missiles

Special Rules:
- Missile Lock
- Strafing Run
- Unrelenting Hunter

Options:
- May replace its twin-linked lascannon with an avenger mega bolter ....*free*

RAVENWING DARK TALON — 160 Points

	Armour BS	F	S	R	HP	Unit Type	UnitComposition	Page
Ravenwing Dark Talon	4	11	11	11	3	Vehicle (Flyer)	1 Ravenwing Dark Talon	51

Wargear:
- Two hurricane bolters
- Rift cannon
- Stasis bomb

Special Rules:
- Hover Strike

Heavy Support

DEVASTATOR SQUAD — 70 Points

	WS	BS	S	T	W	I	A	Ld	Sv	Unit Type	Unit Composition	Page
Space Marine	4	4	4	4	1	4	1	8	3+	Infantry	4 Space Marines	35
Space Marine Sergeant	4	4	4	4	1	4	1	8	3+	Infantry (Character)	1 Space Marine Sergeant	
Veteran Sergeant	4	4	4	4	1	4	2	9	3+	Infantry (Character)		

Wargear:
- Power armour
- Boltgun
- Bolt pistol
- Frag grenades
- Krak grenades
- Signum (Sergeants only)

Special Rules:
- And They Shall Know No Fear
- Combat Squads
- Grim Resolve

Options:
- May include up to five additional Space Marines .... *14 pts/model*
- Up to four Space Marines may replace their boltguns with one of the following:
  - Heavy bolter.................................. *10 pts/model*
  - Multi-melta.................................. *10 pts/model*
  - Missile launcher (with frag and krak missiles) .... *15 pts/model*
    - May also take flakk missiles ...... *10 pts/model*
  - Plasma cannon.............................. *15 pts/model*
  - Lascannon.................................... *20 pts/model*
- May upgrade the Space Marine Sergeant to a Veteran Sergeant................................ *10 pts*
- The Space Marine Sergeant or Veteran Sergeant may take items from the **Melee Weapons** and/or **Ranged Weapons** sections of the wargear list.
- The Space Marine Sergeant or Veteran Sergeant may take melta bombs.... *5 pts*
- May select a Drop Pod, Rhino, or Razorback as a Dedicated Transport (pg 100).

PREDATOR — 75 Points

	BS	Armour F	Armour S	Armour R	HP	Unit Type	Unit Composition	Page
Predator	4	13	11	10	3	Vehicle (Tank)	1 Predator	39

Wargear:
- Autocannon
- Searchlight
- Smoke launchers

Options:
- May replace autocannon with a twin-linked lascannon .... *25 pts*
- May take two side sponsons which are both armed with one of the following:
  - heavy bolters .... *20 pts*
  - lascannons.. *40 pts*
- May take items from the **Dark Angels Vehicle Equipment** list.

WHIRLWIND — 65 Points

	BS	Armour F	Armour S	Armour R	HP	Unit Type	Unit Composition	Page
Whirlwind	4	11	11	10	3	Vehicle (Tank)	1 Whirlwind	39

Wargear:
- Whirlwind multiple missile launcher
- Searchlight
- Smoke launchers

Options:
- Whirlwinds may take items from the **Dark Angels Vehicle Equipment** list.

VINDICATOR — 125 Points

	BS	Armour F	Armour S	Armour R	HP	Unit Type	Unit Composition	Page
Vindicator	4	13	11	10	3	Vehicle (Tank)	1 Vindicator	39

Wargear:
- Demolisher cannon
- Storm bolter
- Searchlight
- Smoke launchers

Options:
- May take items from the **Dark Angels Vehicle Equipment** list.
- May take a siege shield.. *10 pts*

HEAVY SUPPORT

LAND RAIDER — 250 Points

	BS	Armour F	Armour S	Armour R	HP	Unit Type	Unit Composition	Page
Land Raider	4	14	14	14	4	Vehicle (Tank, Transport)	1 Land Raider	41

Wargear:
- Twin-linked heavy bolter
- Two twin-linked lascannons
- Searchlight
- Smoke launchers

Special Rules:
- Assault Vehicle
- Power of the Machine Spirit

Transport Capacity:
- Ten models

Options:
- May take items from the **Dark Angels Vehicle Equipment** list.
- May take a multi-melta .... *10 pts*
- If selected as a Dedicated Transport for a Deathwing Terminator Squad, Deathwing Command Squad or a unit of Deathwing Knights, it must be upgraded to a Deathwing Vehicle (pg 40) .... *30 pts*

LAND RAIDER CRUSADER — 250 Points

	BS	Armour F	Armour S	Armour R	HP	Unit Type	Unit Composition	Page
Land Raider Crusader	4	14	14	14	4	Vehicle (Tank, Transport)	1 Land Raider Crusader	41

Wargear:
- Twin-linked assault cannon
- Two hurricane bolters
- Frag assault launchers
- Searchlight
- Smoke launchers

Special Rules:
- Assault Vehicle
- Power of the Machine Spirit

Transport Capacity:
- Sixteen models

Options:
- May take items from the **Dark Angels Vehicle Equipment** list.
- May take a multi-melta .... *10 pts*
- If selected as a Dedicated Transport for a Deathwing Terminator Squad, Deathwing Command Squad or a unit of Deathwing Knights, it must be upgraded to a Deathwing Vehicle (pg 40) .... *30 pts*

LAND RAIDER REDEEMER — 245 Points

	BS	Armour F	Armour S	Armour R	HP	Unit Type	Unit Composition	Page
Land Raider Redeemer	4	14	14	14	4	Vehicle (Tank, Transport)	1 Land Raider Redeemer	41

Wargear:
- Twin-linked assault cannon
- Two flamestorm cannons
- Frag assault launchers
- Searchlight
- Smoke launchers

Special Rules:
- Assault Vehicle
- Power of the Machine Spirit

Transport Capacity:
- Twelve models

Options:
- May take items from the **Dark Angels Vehicle Equipment** list.
- May take a multi-melta .... *10 pts*
- If selected as a Dedicated Transport for a Deathwing Terminator Squad, Deathwing Command Squad or a unit of Deathwing Knights, it must be upgraded to a Deathwing Vehicle (pg 40) .... *30 pts*

LAND SPEEDER VENGEANCE — 140 Points

	BS	Armour F	Armour S	Armour R	HP	Unit Type	Unit Composition	Page
Land Speeder Vengeance	4	10	10	10	2	Vehicle (Fast, Skimmer)	1 Land Speeder Vengeance	48

Wargear:
- Heavy bolter
- Plasma storm battery

Special Rules:
- Deep Strike

Options:
- A Land Speeder Vengeance may replace its heavy bolter with an assault cannon .... *20 pts*